SMILE JESUS LOVES YOU!

Augusto L. Perez

All scripture references are taken from the King James Version of the Bible.

SMILE JESUS LOVES YOU!
ISBN 978-0967847320

All scripture references are taken from the King James Version of the Bible.

Published by:
Augusto L. Perez

For information on bookings or to place an order please contact us at:

The Appearance Ministries, Inc.
P.O. Box 465
Live Oak, FL. 32064
Web Address: www.theappearance.com

DEDICATION

I dedicate this book to my father and mother Maroel
and Adelaida, who have gone on to be with the Lord.
The lessons and principles they taught me, more by
deeds than by words, still live on in my life. I am
forever grateful to them for the strength, moral
support and love that they always gave to me.
May the Lord reward you for your kindness,
longsuffering and love towards me.

I was blessed to have you as
my mother and father
I love you.

ACKNOWLEDGEMENTS

I want to thank my wonderful Father and Lord Jesus Christ, whom
I love with all my heart, and the precious Holy Spirit. Thank you
for helping me and being with me during the fiery trials,
and using me in spite of my faults and weaknesses.
I could have never made it without you.
I adore you!

To my wife Yvette for your willingness to sacrifice all and to live
with me in rather difficult conditions, at times abject poverty
and loneliness when I had to be on the road, so that
I could obey the call of God in my life.
I love you!

To Lewis Morley, my spiritual father and mentor, who believed
in me when no one else did, birthed me into the ministry and
taught me many things that I still hold close to my heart.
I honor you!

To all the pastors, friends and churches that believed in me,
blessed and supported my ministry, and to this day
are very closely connected to us.
I value you!

To all our dear friends, too numerous to name them all, who have
stood with us in prayer and supported us with their offerings,
so that we can continue winning souls for the Kingdom
and training and equipping the Bride of Christ.
I thank you!

Table of Contents

Chapter 1

THE TELEGRAM

It was a hot, breezy typical summer night in Havana, Cuba in 1963. Like most homes in the neighborhood, we had the front door and the windows open to allow the evening fresh air to come in and cool the house. I was sitting in the living room watching my favorite program "Robin Hood" on our old black and white TV set, when suddenly the relative calm was abruptly interrupted by a man shouting in a very loud voice: "Telegrama!" As we all rushed outside, there riding a new Chinese bicycle was a uniformed young man holding a telegram in his hand. "Official telegram from the Cuban government!" he said in Spanish, as we all stood there without saying a word.

We had never before received a telegram, let alone one from the Cuban government. It was very unusual for telegrams to be delivered at night, especially one that is delivered by a uniformed officer. Needless to say, we were concerned. Many times in the past I had seen men who had a bit too much to drink in the bar next to our home, which was also a grocery store, taken to the "Jefatura" (Police Station) just because they had been blabbing away against the Castro government.

Soon after Fidel Castro had declared in 1960 during one of his notorious long speeches that he was a Communist/Marxist/Leninist, he created and installed "Comites de Defensa de la Revolución" (Committees in Defense of the Revolution, referred to as CDR from now on) on each block to be the eyes and ears of the Cuban Revolution. Castro had come into power in Cuba in 1959 by overturning the corrupt regime of Fulgencio Batista through a revolution that started in Sierra Maestra, a mountainous region on the eastern peninsula of Cuba.

In the beginning of the Cuban revolution, Fidel Castro had the backing and approval of the Cuban people. When he came to Havana from Sierra Maestra with a dove on his shoulder, the people praised him as a savior. Women idolized him so much that they would preserve the soda bottles that Fidel drank from and would worship him as a god. Some women that were kissed by Castro would not wash their mouth for days. He was received with open arms as the Cuban people were happy to see Batista go. During the Batista regime Cuba had become very corrupt, especially in Havana. Abortion clinics, adultery, fornication, drugs, homosexuality, prostitution, gambling casinos, drinking and idolatry just to name a few, had become rampant. Back in the 1950's, when people in the U.S. wanted to do some gambling, they did not go to Las Vegas, they went to the beautiful casinos in Cuba. When men wanted to buy cheap drugs and have a good time with prostitutes in some of the most gorgeous beaches in the world at a reasonable price, they went to Cuba. When the women in the U.S. wanted to have an abortion performed without any problems or hassles with the authorities, they went to Cuba and had it done there for a very low cost and reasonable safety.

Cuba had a reputation of having some of the best doctors and hospital facilities in the world. Even today, after almost forty seven years of Communism that has destroyed the economy, brought deterioration to the infrastructure of the nation and hospitals due to the embargos, and caused a shortage of food, medicine clothing and just about everything else, Cuba still has excellent doctors and many people from all over the world go there to be treated by them.

To this day I believe that it was God that placed Fidel Castro and Communism over the Island of Cuba because of all the things I mentioned above. Even today, though many people have embraced Christianity, the Protestant faith and Pentecostalism in particular, the unbelievers in Cuba remain some of the most idolatrous people in the western hemisphere with the exception of Haiti.

In all my years of travel to many different Latin American countries and cities within the U.S. with large Hispanic populations, I have never encountered a more idolatrous and difficult people to evangelize than the Cuban people. However, once they are saved, they make excellent Christians since they are by nature very warm, compassionate, intelligent and industrious.

Miami, Florida is a perfect example. Back in the early fifties, Miami (and most of Florida) was a vacation spot known mostly for its many sandy beaches, and as the retirement destination for many older people. When the Cuban immigrants started arriving in Miami in the early sixties, they started many businesses that to this day remain as some of the most prosperous in the area: restaurants, pharmacies, grocery stores, banks, hotels, factories, medical centers, construction companies and many others. These businesses became the engine that fueled the economy and the growth of South Florida. And like they say, the rest is history.

The Bay of Pigs Invasion

In 1960 under Operation Zapata, the CIA began to recruit, train and equip Cuban exiles in Guatemala for an armed invasion into Cuba. This was all done with the planning and funding of the U.S. government under the John F. Kennedy administration. The plan was for the Cuban troops to penetrate and invade Cuba at a time when Castro's military was still not strong enough. Once there, American planes would fly in and bomb enemy targets while dropping ammunition and supplies.

However, what took place at the Bay of Pigs invasion was not supposed to happen. As the invading Cuban forces were fighting and pushing back Castro's military, the American planes were ordered to make a U-turn and go back to their bases. The Cuban invading army seeing that they had been left to fend on their own, and with no supplies and ammunition left, were forced to surrender.

Hundreds were tried for treason and executed in prisons throughout Cuba in retaliation for the invasion. All the prisoners were taken to an old prison in the northern coast of Havana called "El Principe", where they remained for well over a year. This was a crushing defeat to the hopes and aspirations of millions of Cubans both in America as well as in Cuba.

The reason I am privy to this information is because my cousin was one of the commanding officers that led the Bay of Pigs invasion in 1961, and later went on to become a Lieutenant Colonel in the United States Army during the Viet Nam war. His father, who was still in Cuba, was told by relatives in the U.S. that his son was involved in the invasion. When we saw his name in the list of captured prisoners released by the government in Cuban, we were very relieved to know he was still alive.

Only women and children were allowed to visit the prisoners in "El Principe". Since the only woman relative he had in Cuba was my mom, she and I were the only ones that were allowed to visit him. We were asked by the prison authorities to supply two canary yellow T-shirts for him to wear. Since my mom was not able to find any, she had to dye two white ones to canary yellow.

We were allowed to visit him once every few weeks, and it was not a pleasant experience for my mother. She would be asked to strip, and searched again and again by female officers. We were exposed to ridicule, mocking and jeering by other common criminals imprisoned there. I will never forget the things that I experienced during this time of my life. It will be forever be indelibly etched in the deepest recesses of my soul.

After twenty months of diplomatic dialogue, all the prisoners were exchanged to the U.S. for $53 million in food and medicine. Cuba was never the same again after that. All the private weapons were confiscated from the population by the Cuban government. It would become a nation obsessed with the revolution, arms and weapons.

4

Castro started using most of the resources in Cuba to buy weapons and military equipment from the Soviet Union at an incredible pace. Eventually Russia started to ship missiles into Cuba, upsetting the balance of power in the region and leading to the infamous October Crisis of 1962 between Nikita Khrushchev and John F. Kennedy. Cuba remains to this day in the western hemisphere, as a nation having one of the strongest military force.

Time to Leave Cuba

As the economic and social conditions worsened in Cuba, many people started leaving by the boatloads. Back in 1960, Cuba still had relations with the U.S. and the price to travel ninety miles across the Gulf between two countries was only twenty five dollars. My twenty year old brother realizing that the walls were quickly closing in on him, and that if he stayed there he could be stuck for good because of his military age, started to do all the necessary paperwork in order to be able to leave the country sometime in 1961.

We had a distant relative living in New Jersey that was willing to take my brother into her home, if he could get his visa and leave the country. After much toil, money and effort, he was able to get his passport, U.S. visa and permission from the Cuban government to leave the country. However, in spite of all the good news he was not prepared for what was about to happen.

A year before, he had sold his 1951 Studebaker car that since he bought it, had brought him nothing but trouble and heartache. Now, as he was attempting to leave the country to travel to America, the government informed him that if he wanted to leave Cuba, he would have to drive his old Studebaker car to the Airport, park it there and give the keys to them.

You see, one of the first reforms the Cuban Revolution had passed when Castro came into power and declared that he was a communist, was to confiscate and take over the money and possessions of the middle class and affluent and give it to those that were in the military or the poor that were sympathetic to the government.

Anyone wanting to leave the country could do so, but not without surrendering everything they owned. You could only take one change of clothing and the clothes on your back. With the help and assistance of the CDR, the Cuban government was able to confiscate everything you had, even possessions you had in the past. They could make you get back whatever you had or replace it with another one just like it, even if it was old and broken down or had just plainly stopped working.

With no idea of where the proud owner of this blessed car was living at the time, my brother started the search. Leaving no stone unturned and through much hard work, he eventually located the man and told him he wanted to buy the car back. Except that the man who was no fool, seeing the predicament that my brother was in, took advantage of the situation and asked for twice as much as he had paid for it a year before.

However, there was no other alternative if my brother was to leave the country. We had already used every nickel and dime we had, and now we had to come up with a large sum of money we did not have. All he had left was his gold watch and that would only pay for a fraction of what the man was asking for. Fortunately my uncle, who we lovingly called "Corucho", put up the rest of the money towards the purchase of the famous car.

The great anticipated day of departure came, but as he tried to start the car to drive it to the airport, it stalled. Everyone with any mechanic abilities in the barrio was summoned in order to get the prodigious car to start. Finally, after a good scare and much sweat and tears, the old Studebaker started. We kissed, hugged and waved good bye as my brother made his way to the great nation of the United States of America.

My brother was one of the last ones to leave Cuba by means of a direct flight from Havana to Miami in 1961, as the United States broke relations with Cuba in the year 1962. We did not know if we would ever see him again. But one thing we knew for sure; this was the right thing to do; little did we know at the time, that three years later we would join him in States.

My Jamaican English Teacher

After the revolution, there were no longer any private or Christian schools in the country since the government had confiscated and taken over all of them. My mother had become increasingly concerned about what they were teaching the children in the government run schools. Like every other country in the world that has embraced communism, Cuba had become quite atheistic and very agnostic. There was no room for God in the Revolution.

In 1962 rumors had begun to spread about the things that were taking place in the school classrooms. The teacher would ask the children to close their eyes and pray to God for some ice cream. After a few moments of muttered prayers by the children, they were told to open their eyes to discover that there was, of course, no ice cream there. Then the teacher again told the children to close their eyes and this time ask Fidel Castro for ice cream. As the children again muttered their innocent prayers asking Fidel for ice cream, the assistants quickly would place small ice cream cups in front of each student.

This and many other forms of indoctrination were used by the government to slowly but consistently turn the hearts of the children from God and parents towards Fidel Castro and the revolution. When the children got to the age of thirteen, they were taken from their parents and enrolled in a program called "Pioneros de la Revolución" (Pioneers of the Revolution). There they would remain until they were well past their teen age years.

I had just turned eleven years old when my mother and father decided that it would be in my best interests to leave Cuba soon. They wanted to send me alone to the U.S. but I was reluctant to leave them behind. I told them that either we would all leave, or none of us would leave. It was then they decided we would all leave Cuba.

My mother made up her mind that she would not send me to one of the government run schools and allow me to be brainwashed and eventually taken away from her, but instead she was going to find me a private teacher who would teach me to speak, read and write English and prepare me for our eventual trip to the United States.

Back then, there were many people from all over the world that were living in Cuba. The Cuban people had a way of embracing them and making them feel at home. They had come to live there from Spain, China, Poland, Germany, America, England, Israel, Japan, Lebanon, Russia, Poland, France and Jamaica just to name a few.

Someone recommended to my mother this Jamaican teacher who lived a block away from where we lived. She agreed to teach me English for a couple of hours, three times a week in her own home for a small fee. This would have to be done secretly and carefully, so as to avoid been seen by the watchful eyes of the CDR in our block. I was not to talk about it, share anything about it with no one or trust anyone no matter how well we knew them.

I found a way to get to her house through the back alleys of the houses in our block, and would stealthfully make my way there three times a week without being seen by any member of the CDR. This required a high degree of strategy, cunning and wisdom on my part. To this day I am amazed at how I was able to pull this off without being seen. For sure, it must have been the hand of God protecting me and guiding me.

On the days that I was not learning English, I would go with my father and help him do his work. Back then he worked for a car insurance company and the bills were not collected through the mail like in this country, but he went personally to their homes and collected it from them. More work but less delinquent bills that way.

Gertrude was the name of my Jamaican English teacher, I still remember it well. She was really a very nice lady and with time became very attached to me. Even years after I had left Cuba, she would still write me letters and ask if everything was all right. She was always concerned about my safety and well being to the point where many times she would even give me her own food so that I would not go hungry.

Life in Communist Cuba

You see after Cuba turned Communist, everything was rationed by the government due to the U.S. embargo. They issued a ration card to every family specifying how much of each item they were to receive weekly, monthly or yearly. For example, we were allowed a pound of coffee and five pounds of sugar once a month. Items like chicken and eggs, which we were supposed to get once a week, we would only get it whenever they were available, which was only once every four to six weeks.

Whenever an item arrived at the local grocery store or pharmacy, long lines would immediately form to receive your quota of food. Usually there was not enough to give to all the people present, and those at the end of the line went away empty handed. It was terrible to see so many old people and families with their children go away with nothing after standing in line for hours.

Things like red meat would be even scarcer, and we would get it only once every few months. Milk was only given to children under the age of six. If there were no children of that age, you would not get any milk. Clothing items were not too bad, except for shoes. The only shoes available were Russian and Czechoslovakian shoes which were very hard and uncomfortable. Medicine was the hardest of all to get, since Cuba always imported most of its medicine from America, along with many other items.

When the U.S. enacted an embargo against Cuba in 1962, all the medicine, medical equipment, food, cars, supplies, raw materials and most other items had to be imported from the Soviet Union, China and communist bloc nations which were all the way in Europe. The Cuban economy, which before the communist revolution was strong and robust and depended mostly on good sugar cane harvests, now had become very sluggish.

One of the reasons that Communism does not work is because it does not provide an incentive for people. The only reason that human beings work and sacrifice is simply because they expect to get something in return. Whether it is money, privileges, a better life or whatever, people are always motivated by some kind of incentive. No one likes to sacrifice and do things for free, especially if it is imposed on you by force.

Communism levels the playing field in a country so that everyone makes about the same, and receives the same benefits no matter what they do; that is everyone but the ruling class in the government. The rules do not apply to them. People like doctors, for example, make just slightly more money than a carpenter, plumber or garbage collector, which is the equivalent of about twenty five dollars a month.

This type of a system is not conducive for economic growth in a country, causing stagnation and eventually leading to poverty and hunger in the masses. One of the things that make America so great is its constitution, which states that every human being is endowed by God with certain inalienable rights and freedoms. That is exactly what Communism takes away from the people.

What Communism attempts to do in the flesh using force can only be achieved through a genuine conversion to Jesus Christ by allowing Him to fill you with His love and compassion. The principles found in early Christian Church society (Acts 2:44-47) embody many of the same principles you find in Socialism, except that it was always done voluntarily and out of love; not by force, ambition jealousy, greed and hatred in their hearts.

I remember one morning after the CDR had done one of its many marches around the barrio chanting their patriotic songs the evening before, we found a toy worm literally hanging from our door. You see, anyone who did not sympathize with the Castro regime was considered a worm by his followers and the CDR. They were relentless in their attacks and threats against anyone that did not sympathize with and support the revolution.

We knew that staying in Cuba was not an option. My father started getting all the paperwork ready so that we could leave to the United States as soon as possible. The U.S. no longer had diplomatic relations with Cuba, so we had to find another way. One of the few non-communist nations that still had relations with Cuba back then was Spain. So the people started to go to Spain, and from there they would try to make it eventually into the U.S.

Getting the government's permission to leave Cuba soon became our quest for the Golden Fleece. It seemed like they had us going in circles. The bureaucratic red tape kept getting harder and harder to cut through. My dad had spent most of his money on government and attorney fees. Now after two years, we were starting to get weary, depressed and at the point of loosing hope.

As a last resort and at the risk of loosing everything, my mother decided to talk to a distant relative who was a high member of the Communist Party and worked in the Department of the Interior. To our own surprise, he was very understanding and compassionate, and promised us that he would do everything in his power to look for our application for a permit to leave Cuba, and push it through the appropriate channels. All that remained now was pray and hope that he would be successful.

"Are you Maroel Perez?" asked the young uniformed officer in Spanish. "Please sign here!" As my dad nodded and signed the paper nervously, the young man left in his Chinese bicycle leaving the telegram in the trembling hand of my father. As he quickly opened it, he read it out loud: "You are hereby notified that permission to leave Cuba has been granted to (our names). Please report to the Department of the Interior as soon as possible." It was a miracle; finally we were leaving Cuba.

Chapter 2

TO SPAIN WITH LOVE

The departure date we were given to leave Cuba by the Department of the Interior was December 23, 1963, which gave us several months for us to get the smallpox vaccine and take care of other things required by immigration. As we started to prepare for our trip to Spain, my mom and dad realized we were going to a place much colder than we were used to.

We had never experienced any weather colder than 50 degrees Fahrenheit and then only for a few days. Now for the first time in our lives, we were going to be in a place that was much colder than that and we did not have any appropriate clothing for that kind of weather.

My father had used all the money trying to get us out of Cuba, and only had enough money left to buy a winter coat for my mom. I guess his reasoning was that we men would have to tough it out somehow once we got to Spain. Latin men strongly believe in the "macho" thing you know. I know that the women's Liberation Movement has changed a lot of that and it is not in style, but I kind of miss some of the old fashioned ways and traditions.

I still give up my seat to the opposite sex, open doors for my wife, and pick up things she drops to the floor. I still believe women are the weaker vessel and it is the gentlemanly thing to do, but unfortunately this belief is not shared by most in the world today. As a matter of fact, they look at you funny if you do stuff like that.

Today women do un-lady like things like fight in the army, work in construction jobs, drive taxis, fly jets, arm wrestle, and work nine to five jobs alongside men while a Daycare looks after the children. I guess that times have changed, and this is just the way it is in the twenty first century, but I was taught differently by my parents, and was brought up in a much different environment.

Where is the TV Set?

One day, as we were making the final arrangements to leave the country, we were paid a visit by the woman leader of the local CDR, along with a policeman. They started to check our home, making an inventory of everything we had on a piece of paper. Suddenly, with a frown on her face the woman asked: "didn't you have a black and white television in your home?" All of a sudden, I sensed the atmosphere get very tense.

My parents tried to explain to her that it was a very old unit and that it had just quit on us. Many times before it had done the exact same thing but it had been technically resurrected by a TV technician friend of ours. So now when it broke a few weeks earlier, they decided to just get rid of it since we were leaving the country. This was not received very well by the woman who immediately said: "Well, you are just going to have to replace it!"

You see, if you wanted to leave Cuba, you had to leave everything you owned to the government, including things you may have had in the past. You could not take jewelry, money, watches, rings or anything else. If you owned property, it was confiscated by the government. You were only allowed to take one change of clothing and the clothes on your back.

Fortunately for us, our technician friend happened to have an old black and white TV just like the one we had in his shop that he could let us have for nothing. Once we replaced our black and white TV, we were cleared by the CDR and the police department to leave the country.

The Day of Departure

From the moment my brother got to the U.S. he did nothing but work and save the money so he could pay for all the expenses of our trip from Cuba to Spain and then from Spain to the United States. When we informed him that we had received a telegram giving us permission to leave the country, he quickly sent us the money to purchase our airline tickets to Spain. His unselfish acts of love and kindness towards us and God's great grace are the only reasons I am in this nation today.

My dad purchased the airline tickets with the money we received from my brother, and started to get ready for the day of departure. I had sold most of my games and toys earlier in 1963, just before the January 6 Cuban Holiday "Dia de los Reyes Magos", Spanish for "The Day of the Magi" which is the equivalent of Christmas day in the U.S. where the children receive games and toys from their parents. My parents sold a few items, but we gave away most of our belongings to our family and friends.

Finally the day before our departure, the CDR came and inspected our house to make sure everything was there. After they were satisfied, we were asked to step outside our home and they sealed it with a government seal. No one was allowed to go back in once the seal was in place. My uncle Corucho, who was waiting for us outside, drove us to his home where we spent the night.

The next day we rose up early, and he drove us to Rancho Boyeros Airport. On the way to the Airport, my mother asked Corucho to drive us by our home so we could look at it one last time. Outside the home waiting for us were our little dog and our cat Miliciano thinking we would return soon to take care of them. When we got to the Airport we hugged, kissed and cried as we said our good byes. My uncle Corucho, who we loved dearly, had been there for us all along; little did we know that this would be the last time that we would see him or talk to him. He died one year later of a heart attack.

As we went inside the airport, we were taken to these rooms and asked to strip. There in separate rooms, they checked us in every nook and cranny to make sure we were not trying to smuggle something out of the country. Afterwards, the government militia checked our baggage item by item, again looking for any suspicious signs that would indicate to them we were smuggling anything out of the country. They would have immediately stopped us from leaving the country at the slightest sign of trouble, and we would have been unable to protest or argue at all.

When they were satisfied that we were all "clean", we were allowed to go to the gate from where the plane would depart. There we had to wait a long time before being told to start boarding the plane. However, when we were about halfway through the boarding process, the authorities stopped it and ordered the people to get off the plane. We saw the authorities come and take a few people away to be interrogated by the secret police. This was done twice right in front of our eyes. Needless to say, everyone was terrified thinking they would be next.

Finally, everyone was allowed to board the plane, the seat belts were fastened and the overhead compartments closed. Suddenly, as the plane was ready to move out for takeoff, the pilot received a notice from the Cuban authorities informing him that there was a problem, and the passengers would have to come down from the plane once again. The pilot however, was incensed and refused to comply with this last order stating that the plane had been cleared for takeoff, and he would not allow it. The Cuban government had no choice but to allow the plane to finally take off and leave with its passengers for Spain.

As the plane took off and it became evident to all the passengers that we were in the air on our way to Spain, a great uproar could be heard throughout the plane as the people started crying, laughing and shouting "Somos Libres" (We Are Free). It was hard to believe that finally we were leaving behind such suffering, persecution and oppression. We had been given the most precious gift a human being can have; the freedom to live his life as he desires, and the right to the pursuit of happiness.

These are the two most cherished rights that make the United States of America one of the greatest nations in the world to live in. That is the reason why millions of people all over the world have sought in past times to come here. When the American people no longer cherish these inalienable rights and freedom is taken away from them, this nation will cease to be great.

How could this happen to any nation? Such a thing could never happen in America. Or could it? All it takes is for people to forget about God, and allow corruption to begin to defile their land until a nation is transformed little by little in every level of society. This is exactly what happened in Cuba, and sadly no one was aware of what was happening, until it was too late.

The Cuban people placed their confidence, trust and hope in a man, attributing to him messianic qualities that should be reserved only for Jesus Christ. People thought that Castro would bring utopia to Cuba through change, but instead he brought a terrible oppressive dictatorship. They soon learned that promises are made easily, but keeping them is much harder. As the saying goes, those that do not learn from history are doomed to repeat it.

Spain Welcomes Us

On our way to Spain, we made two stops for refueling in Bermuda and Azores. The plane we were flying on was one of the old DC3 propeller aircraft. It took us twenty six hours to fly to Spain from Cuba. We left on the morning of December 23, 1963 and arrived at Madrid International Airport on the afternoon of December 24.

When we arrived, the Red Cross was waiting for us and gave every passenger in the plane that did not have one a winter coat. It was a very cold afternoon in Madrid, and the Cuban people were not used to such severe weather, as the weather in Cuba is tropical. We all got our coats and proceeded to the Customs office.

On the way there, I noticed that the people were looking at me kind of strange. When I asked my parents if there was something wrong, my father said to me in Spanish: "They gave you a woman's coat". Sure enough, when I looked in the mirror I realized that in the rush to get our coats and go to the Customs office, I had been given a woman's coat. Well, I was not about to freeze to death so I had not choice but to wear it, along with a funny looking winter hat they gave me.

On the Way to Jacometrezo

All the Cuban refugees were told to go to a Catholic Relief Center called "Jacometrezo" just a few blocks away where we would receive help and direction. As we made our way to this office, we walked several blocks and there was no sign of Jacometrezo. Before we left Cuba, my dad had bought me a new pair of shoes from Czechoslovakia which were as hard as rocks and were torture on my feet.

As my feet started to hurt and bleed, I began limping very badly with my woman's coat and weird looking hat. It was quite a spectacle. Seeing the predicament I was in, my father volunteered to switch shoes and let me wear his American shoes, while he would take on the forsaken Czechoslovakian shoes. Wearing the same size of shoes as my dad proved to be quite a blessing for me.

Needless to say, I was quite overwhelmed with joy and relief. My dad however, was quite a different story. After a few blocks, he quickly started limping badly as the Czechoslovakian shoes did their deadly work on his feet. His pain and agony were quite noticeable on his face; bless his heart. After getting lost several times, we finally made it to Jacometrezo. We were given twenty dollars (One thousand, two hundred pesetas) and told to go to a cheap motel nearby.

Our New Temporary Home

The name of the motel was "Hostal de Viajeros". As we arrived at the motel, the first thing we noticed was an old fashioned wooden elevator that looked more like a wooden coffin than an elevator. As we got into this elevator, we were informed by the man operating it that we could only use it to go up, not down. To come down we had to come down three flights of stairs.

After what seemed like an eternity, we arrived at the third floor and quickly got off the elevator. We were all welcomed into the motel by a woman who turned out to be the manager. She led us through this long, dimly lit hall with loose floor tiles that made a horrible clapping sound as you walked on them. When we finally arrived to our room, we found two old beds with a simple night stand, however we saw no bathroom.

When we finished unpacking, we inquired one of the guests where the bathroom was. They took us to this huge bathroom, and as we started checking it we noticed that there was no hot water. When we inquired, we were told that there was no hot water, and that we would have to take our showers in the public showers available at the main subway station in Madrid.

Needless to say, with freezing temperatures in Madrid, we had to find other means of providing hot water. After a few days we received some money which our brother had wired to us and we went out shopping for some food, as well as the means to heat our water. The only stoves that were available were very expensive, and our budget was very limited. We had to keep on looking.

Finally after much searching, my mother found this small cast iron device called "Infiernillo" in a small convenience store which worked really well. She filled it with alcohol, lit it with a match and began to heat some water in a small bucket we had bought. We were on our way to finally being able to bathe.

We took turns to wash ourselves in the room with a small towel and soap. My father however, was not able to adjust to the tedious technique involved in taking baths with small towels and a bucket, and rather opted to go and take his showers in the public bathrooms located in the main subway station in Plaza del Sol.

With time, we found out that the owners of the hotel were not too fond of taking showers. They would skip bathing for two or three days without batting an eye. Whether this was because of choice or necessity, I do not know, although I have my suspicions. As a result, those around them had to pay the price through their noses.

The Soup Kitchen

We tried our best to buy and eat those items which were good and cheap in the country of Spain. For example, you could buy a whole bunch of olives, some apples and a couple of loaves of bread for less than two hundred "Pesetas", the national currency of Spain. One U.S. Dollar would get you seventy Pesetas. My father also bought some ham and cheese and my mother made some real good sandwiches.

However, we realized that we were not going to have enough money to be able to eat like this every day due to our very limited budget. One of the other Cubans staying at the same Hotel told us that we could eat a free lunch and dinner Monday through Saturday at a Catholic soup kitchen located at Plaza Mayor. We decided we would check it out, and maybe start eating at the soup kitchen.

We took the Subway and made three connections to get to the soup kitchen from our hotel. The subway fare was only one peseta, which when you calculate it comes out to less than one cent. Most people in Spain took the subway to get around. Very few people had a private car like they did in the States. Yet the people seemed happy.

When we finally arrived at the soup kitchen, we had to stand in line in the freezing cold weather until the doors opened. When we finally went inside, we sat in these long tables that could sit about twenty people on both sides. Each table had several baskets of bread and a few pitchers of water. As we sat down, the chief nun that ran the soup kitchen would stand in front of us and lead us in a prayer to bless the food.

The lunch was usually pretty good, consisting mostly of bean soup, rice, salad and sometimes fried fish. On the evening, whatever was left from lunch would be used for dinner, usually in the form of a soup. I never heard anybody complain, as they were all thankful to have some food to put in our bellies.

On our way back to the hotel, we always passed this pastry shop which had the most delicious desserts on display. Finally one day, my mother could not resist the temptation any longer and she went inside and bought a vanilla cream filled pastry called "pepito" for each of us. Since then, we stopped by on our way back from the soup kitchen, and everyone had a pepito for dessert.

Most of the guests at the hotel were Cuban people that had fled the Castro regime in Cuba. Every evening after dinner, most of the people would gather in the large living room around the fireplace and talk about their personal experiences in Cuba and life in general. Often, a Spaniard military man staying at the hotel would join us and start singing old sentimental ballads with his guitar as the people applauded and had a great time.

Soon afterwards, a young heavy set Cuban man revealed to us that he was a professional singer in Cuba. After some persuading, he also started singing every evening and delighting us with beautiful songs. This came to be one of our favorite times of the day as the people loved to spend time together and reminisce about the past. Everybody had a sad story to tell, but it always ended up with everyone rejoicing and laughing together.

I shared the story of "Manolo", the proud owner of a little hamburger stand on the corner of "Quinta y Doce", a busy corner where we lived in Havana, Cuba. Before Castro came to power, on weekends I loved to eat his famous "fritas", the Cuban version of the American sausage biscuit. However, after the U.S. embargo when food started becoming scarce, he closed down his shop.

A few weeks later, we noticed that cats around the neighborhood started to disappear one by one. All of a sudden one day out of nowhere, we see Manolo arrive with a basket full of fritas to reopen his hamburger stand. When asked where he got the meat from, he simply said with a smile that miraculously God had provided the beef for his hamburger stand. Needless to say, all the people roared in laughter as I shared the true story.

Spain, the Mother Country

Overall, our time in Spain was a happy one. Every day we went out together and I got to spend a lot of personal time with my mom and dad. We walked through one of the oldest and most famous streets in the city of Madrid "Alcala", as well as "La Gran Via" (The Great Lane). Often we would stop and buy roasted chestnuts from street vendors and eat them as we walked the city.

There were multitudes of people walking in the streets of Madrid at all hours of the day and night. No one was afraid of being mugged or robbed by thugs. We found out that the people in Madrid were very friendly and eager to help us whenever we asked for information or directions. They were very sympathetic to our cause, and generous with their time, sometimes even walking us all the way.

Most of them understood what had taken place in Cuba, because Franco had fought the communists to prevent them from taking over Spain. The police protection was very strong during the Franco regime. He was considered a benign dictator by most. He was very tough on those who broke the law; however everyone was free to live their lives as they saw fit, as long as they did not commit any crimes or cause any trouble.

Policemen with big clubs and guns would patrol the streets on foot, and occasionally you would see a few of them riding on horses through the streets. They were very courteous and respectful. You could tell they were there to serve and protect the people, not like what is beginning to take place in America today where people can get "tazed" by the police at the slightest provocation or any sign of not being fully cooperative with them.

Another thing we noticed was that we were able to go to the pharmacy and buy different antibiotics and other medications without having a doctor's prescription. The pharmacist would offer his expertise to help you get the best medication for your particular ailment. This was the same way it was in Cuba before Castro came into power.

In the United States everything is so controlled by the pharmaceutical industry and the medical profession, that you can barely buy medicine that is any good without a doctor's prescription; and the medicine is so expensive that unless you have a good insurance, you cannot afford it. Today, the FDA together with the big pharmaceutical industry is so powerful that it is threatening to one day maybe stop the sale of vitamins to the public.

What happened to the days when doctors used simple remedies made with natural organic herbs and foods created by God? Most of the people were healed and lived longer, healthier lives. Today most doctors want to heal every disease with drugs and pills made from deadly chemicals, mass produced in huge laboratories. Their true motivation is to line their pockets with money at the expense of the health and welfare of the people.

Although many of these medications may momentarily take care of your particular problem, in the process of doing so it creates a bunch of new problems; these problems then need to be corrected by other prescribed drugs, which in turn create new problems. This process leaves the poor patient in a never-ending death cycle of drugs, eventually leading him to his demise.

The main reason this happens is because most of the time what gets treated by doctors is the symptom, not the root cause. I see this happen all the time in ministry where pastors try to do the same thing. The feelings of depression, oppressions and manifestations of sin in the lives of people cannot be addressed by preaching feel good messages. Although it may placate those feelings momentarily, in the end it only makes matters worse.

Chapter 3

COMING TO AMERICA

During the last month of our three month stay in Spain, we were able to move to a nicer hotel that had a bathroom with hot water. Now we were finally able to take normal showers every day, and everything also was much closer. While in Spain, we noticed that instead of refrigerators, most people had a box sticking out the kitchen window to refrigerate food. Since the climate in Madrid is usually cold at night, it works fine.

After going through much legal due process in the American Embassy, and being told repeatedly by the Spanish liaison that we would never be able to speak to the American ambassador, we got an interview with the Ambassador. We went through a series of never ending questions and answers, and finally were given the visa to be able to enter the United States.

Everyone was very happy and excited. It had been almost three years since we had last seen my brother, and at times we wondered if we would ever see him again. But now, after all we had been through, we were finally coming to America to be reunited with him. He truly had been an exemplary son. Because of his faithfulness and sacrifice, we were going to be able to see our dream come true. My brother sent us the air fare money, and we were able to quickly purchase airline tickets with Iberia for March 7, 1964.

While we waited and prepared for the date of departure, we said our good byes and exchanged information with all of our new made friends. Everyone was happy to see us finally make it to the U.S. Our time in Spain had come to an end. In spite of all the difficulties we had encountered, we all had very good memories of Spain. Now it was time to get ready to come to the great nation of the United States.

The Reunion

After several hours of flight, we arrived at the John F. Kennedy Airport in New York City at night. As the plane made its approach to the city, we saw millions of lights illuminating the night sky. The city that never sleeps is what the notorious singer Frank Sinatra called it in his famous song "New York, New York". Now we were about to land on it and you could feel excitement in the atmosphere of the airplane.

As the plane landed and taxied through the terminal to the appointed gate, everyone collected their belongings and prepared to exit the plane as quickly as possible. As we proceeded to gather our luggage, we were met there by my brother along with several members of our family, who at the time were living in Newark, New Jersey. We hugged and kissed each other as tears rolled down our cheeks. We were finally reunited!

From the airport, a caravan of cars proceeded to take us to my aunt's home where my brother had been living for almost three years. She had been very gracious and kind to allow my brother to stay and live with her for all that time free of charge. Without her help, he probably would have never made it out of Cuba, and neither would we. We brought her from Spain a very expensive hand woven table cloth which made her really happy.

We also brought my brother a beautiful hand made Spanish guitar. My dad who was a classical guitar player, had hand picked this guitar from among dozens of them in a classical guitar shop in Madrid, Spain. Since we were kids, my father taught my brother and me how to play the guitar. We all would spend hours and hours playing the guitar and enjoying each other's company later on.

We spent hours that night in my aunt's house, talking, eating, telling and re-telling the stories of our ordeals in Cuba, Spain and the final trip to America. Everyone there cried, laughed and genuinely loved on each other. When we finally left late at night, we were driven by my uncle to an apartment nearby that my brother had rented for us. It was a real pretty apartment, all furnished.

After we arrived, my brother showed us around the apartment after which we spent some more time talking. I don't think anyone slept much that night; there was so much to talk about. We wanted to make up for lost time, and tried to catch up on everything that was going on in my brother's life. We found out he was working for a toy company distributor as their accountant. The company distributed model toys made by Aurora and Revell.

The company was a few blocks away from where we lived, and since he did not own a car, he had to take a bus to get there every day. A few days later, my father started working there as well in the shipping department. My mother packed lunches for them every day, but sometimes I would walk all the way there to bring them a hot lunch. I didn't mind doing it at all, after all my brother always rewarded me with a model airplane to assemble.

It was too late to enroll me in the school for that year, so I had a lot of free time on my hands. Since my brother got a substantial price discount on the products where he worked, he kept me busy all summer assembling the toy model airplanes, boats and other toys he brought me. I also picked up a pocket Spanish/English dictionary and spent some time learning new words in English as well as brushing up on my grammar and vocabulary.

Going Back to School

As the summer was coming to an end, we were able to move to a nicer place with the extra money coming in from my dad's income. The Italian owners of the new apartment we rented had a son about my age, who attended a private Catholic Elementary School nearby. My parents managed to enroll me in Saint Antoninus School at the grade level that I was supposed to be in.

Ralph, the owner's son, was a great help in teaching me to speak English and serving as my practice partner. He showed me around the school, and introduced me to other students. Because his native language was Italian, which is similar to Spanish, he was able to understand me better than most other students. We became very good friends and spent lots of time together.

Although I had not gone to school for almost two years because of the communist indoctrination in Cuba, I still was pretty sharp in math; however, I struggled with English. I could read it and write it, but when it came to being able to speak it and understand it, that was a totally different matter. Even with my pocket dictionary which I carried with me at all times, it was an exercise in futility whenever I tried to communicate with others.

One time Sister Clarita, the nun in one of my classes, slapped me because she thought I had deliberately disobeyed her, when in fact I had no idea what she was talking to me about. To make matters worse when I tried to defend myself by telling her that I had not understood what she told me, she rebuked me and slapped me again on the other cheek, only this time much harder.

On another occasion, with the help of my trusty pocket dictionary, I tried to tell this girl I really liked in my class, that she was so beautiful I was going to dream about her that night. To my surprise, she opened her blue eyes wide and slapped me. She went and told Sister Clarita, who did not waste any time in making a beeline towards me and slapping me again.

It turned out that instead of using the right word to tell the girl I was going to dream with her that night, in my nervousness I had instead used the word sleep. Needless to say, this incident did not help me at all in gaining self confidence while learning to speak English. However, I was determined to overcome every obstacle and these types of incidents only served to make me study harder and practice more until I mastered the language.

I had to attend summer school that year to become more proficient in reading and comprehension. With time and a lot of hard work, I became better at understanding and speaking the English language. I even began to win prizes (which consisted of statues of saints) for being the best in the class. Also, Sister Clarita did not slap me any more and even started to like me.

The nuns had a habit of keeping us in after lunch in the cafeteria and make us sing to the blessed virgin for a long time. Sometimes, they would take us outside in the yard and make us sing there. Sister Theresa, the head superintendent of the school, told me that I had a great voice and should join the church choir. After consulting with my parents, I joined the church choir and sang there until the time of my graduation.

Uncle Sam Wants You

In 1965 while the Vietnam War was raging hot, the Selective Service sent a letter to my brother requesting him to report immediately to the nearest office and wait for further instructions. When my mom and dad heard of the news, they became afraid and very concerned about our future. We were very concerned for the safety of my brother if he went to go fight in the Vietnam War, plus the fact that he was the main support of the family.

My mother was unable to work because of a chronic disease in her spine, which rendered her useless to do any manual labor. She was continually in pain and had to take pain killers all day long just to be able to move around. My brother had been able to insure her through his job, but even then, the medicines that the doctor prescribed her were very expensive and hard to buy.

A friend of my brother told him that if he could get a letter from a good reputable source like our own Catholic Archdiocese explaining the situation, he would probably get a deferment from Selective Service duty. When I heard this, wanting to do my part and give back a little for all that my brother had done for us, I took it upon myself to go talk to Father Kearny, the head priest in charge of the Catholic Archdiocese where we lived.

When I mentioned to my parents and my brother what I was about to do, they did not take me seriously. After all, I was only thirteen years old and could barely speak the language. However, I have never been one to give up easily on anything in spite of the challenge, opposition or difficulty of the task at hand. I was not about to let my brother be taken and killed in a distant foreign land, fighting an unpopular war for who knows what purpose.

The next day I stepped into the Church office and asked to speak with Father Kearny. I was informed by his secretary that he would be able to see me right away. Armed with my trusty pocket dictionary and a fierce determination, I made my way into his large office and sat in a plush chair across Father Kearny's desk. With a very kind voice he said to me: "How can I help you, son"?

In broken English and with the help of my pocket dictionary, I proceeded to tell Father Kearny, who nodded his head occasionally while listening, how we had just arrived from Cuba through Spain a year before, the predicament that we were in with my brother being called to Selective Service, and how he would be able to help. He waited till I was finished, then told me that he would write the letter and have it ready for me the next day.

The next day when I arrived home from school with the letter from Father Kearny, written on a letterhead from the Newark Archdiocese addressed to the Selective Service Office, my mother and father became extremely happy and very impressed. The letter clearly explained that my brother was the sole provider for our household, my mother's medical condition, and urged that my brother be exempted from Selective Service at this time.

When my brother presented this letter to the Selective Service, he was told that they would review it and inform him of their decision through the mail. After waiting anxiously several weeks for their reply, he finally got a letter from the Selective Service stating that after careful review of his case, he was being granted a deferment in lieu of the extreme hardship that it would cause our family. We had won this battle with God's help, but dark clouds were looming on the horizon.

The Riots Of 66

During my final year at Saint Antoninus Elementary School in the beginning of 1966, my parents moved to an older but much bigger apartment on the second floor of an old furniture store. I had to walk a bit further to get to school but I had my very own bedroom, and even had a small room for all the model airplanes and boats I had put together and painted during the last two years.

This was the time when riots were beginning to take place throughout the country, and there were reports of vandalism, looting and many fires started by mobs of discontented black people who felt oppressed and abused by the government and the white people in general. We were not aware that racism and prejudice was a problem in this country until these things started taking place.

A young black preacher by the name of Martin Luther King had risen to prominence, and his eloquent speeches were stirring deep emotions in the heartland of America. He believed that all people were created equal in the eyes of God, and that men should be judged by the content of their character and not the color of their skin. He was a good man, and a great leader who was mightily used by God to fight inequality and discrimination in this country.

He was a pacifist who used peaceful demonstrations to drive his point home. The many cases of reported riots, fires and vandalism were not instigated by him, but by extreme groups of black Muslims who saw an opening to advance their cause and bring much destruction to cities, and death to the innocent people who lived there. However, Martin Luther King was blamed for most of it, and in the end paid for it with his life.

During the years that I spent in Cuba as a child, I had never seen this type of racism and prejudice exhibited by the Cuban people. Although black slaves were brought to Cuba just like in the United States, after slavery was abolished, blacks and whites lived in harmony with each other. In Cuba, the issue of race would only come to the fore on rare situations, but even then it was nothing like what we saw in America during the 1960's.

I could not believe the horror stories that I have heard about the things that were done to black people, and how they were treated in this country in the past. How a human being can treat another so bad just because of the color of their skin is totally beyond my comprehension. No human being should treat another that way, especially if they are Christians; yet this continues to happen today.

The Fire

I finally graduated from St. Antoninus and proceeded to attend Essex Catholic High School, which was regarded as one of the best high schools in the area. My family wanted to give me the best possible education, and at the same time instill in me Christian principles. I really liked the school and the disciplined way in which it was run. I had to take two buses to get there, but it was worth it.

I had to choose between Latin and Greek in my first year, and I chose to take Latin. I became so good at it, that I went on later to take it for a second year. Most of the teachers were priests, but not all of them. The Latin teacher was very demanding, but an excellent teacher. He made us memorize a bunch of words every day, and we had to pronounce them perfectly. I can still remember some of them to this day.

One night during the time that I was attending this high school in 1967, a great tragedy took place. We had just retired to bed, when all of a sudden my brother saw smoke coming through the wall of his bedroom. Without thinking about it twice, he let out a loud scream "Fire" as he started running throughout the whole place. We were all half sleep, as we got up and threw some clothes on.

By now the fire was coming through the walls, and the smoke had become very thick. We knew we only had a few moments left to be able to escape with our lives. My parents, my brother and I got all our documents, money and the guitar we had brought from Spain and ran down the stairs out to the street. As we stood there watching our home and all our belongings go up in smoke, we could not hold back this empty feeling of sadness.

A short while later, the fire trucks came and after what seemed like the longest time, they managed to put the fire out. Thankfully, no one was harmed in the fire. Now we were on the streets with nothing, but we had each other. This horrible thought began to cross our minds of what would have happened if the fire had taken place much later that night; we could have all perished.

We gathered whatever we could salvage from the fire, and moved in with some of our relatives who lived in a large apartment in the city of Newark, New Jersey. The few clothes we salvaged had this terrible stench no matter how many times we washed it. After a very long investigation, the police determined that the fire was started in the furniture store right below where we lived, and that it was probably arson.

With the financial burden this fire had placed on my family, they were no longer in a position to be able to pay for my private school. The only way I could possibly finish out the year there was for the Catholic Archdiocese to absorb the remaining cost of my tuition. Once again, I went to talk to Father Kearny, and this time I was able to explain the situation to him much easier.

After hearing me out and getting a whiff of the horrible stench coming from my clothes, he took pity on me and agreed to have the Archdiocese absorb the remaining balance of my tuition for that school year. As I walked out of his office, I got the distinct feeling that Father Kearny had seen enough of me, and didn't want to see me again come walking in through the doors of his office.

Time to Move

After living with our relatives for a while, we moved out and rented a furnished apartment in a Portuguese neighborhood where we lived until the end of my school year. My brother and some of my cousins decided to go to Miami for vacation that year, and check out the city as well with their other cousins living there. When they all returned, they came back with a great tan and talking positive about the city and how much fun they had there.

In the meantime, things in the city of Newark, New Jersey continued to get so bad with all the riots and turmoil that two of our related families decided to sell everything they had and move to Miami. At about the same time, some of our long time friends also began moving away, some to California, others to Baltimore, Maryland, and others to Miami, Florida.

We had lived in Newark for three years, and still had some family and many friends there, but somehow it did not feel the same anymore. The terrible experience we had gone through with the fire had left a bad taste in our mouths, let alone our clothes which still reeked with the stench of smoke. My brother also had become unhappy with his job, when the promotion he was promised and was expecting suddenly vanished, along with the raise.

My mother's health also had worsened because of the inclement cold climate. She had rheumatoid arthritis in her spine and neck, which was made worse by all the snow and the cold weather. The warm climate seemed to benefit her and help her to stay active, and thus free of pain. The long harsh winters and the very short summer seasons did not seem to help either.

I noticed that slowly my family began to talk about the possibility of us moving to Miami as well. We figured that if we were ever going to make the move, now was the perfect time. It made a lot of sense, especially since we had lost everything in the fire, and now also most of our family lived there. With my school year now over, we had three full months in the summer that we could use to move and get settled in the city of Miami.

If we waited too long, the new school year would begin and because I could not attend the Essex Catholic High School any longer, my parents would have to make a decision on what public high school to send me to. In addition, then we would have to wait another year to make the move. The more we thought about it, the more convinced we became that now was the time to do it.

With a few nudges from our family in Miami, the decision became easy. We started to communicate with our relatives there, and began to ask probing questions about the job and the housing market. There were not as many job opportunities in the city of Miami as there were in Newark, and the salaries were not as high. Also, the rents were only a tad lower than in Newark. However, we knew that there was no way we would stay in Newark.

We picked a date of departure and started to make all the necessary arrangements. We decided we were going to make the long trip by car in the 1963 Buick that my brother had bought and was in pretty good condition. We calculated that we would have to travel a total of 1,560 miles, and that it would take us two days to get there. My brother would have to do all the driving since my dad did not have license yet, and I was too young to drive.

On the appointed day, we left early in the morning and drove to the city of Baltimore, where we stayed overnight in the home of some friends we had known for years. The man was a psychiatrist who worked in one of the nut houses in the city, and loved to hypnotize people. He asked me a couple of times if I wanted to be hypnotized by him, to which I responded with a resounding NO!

They showed us around the city, and took us to a very old landmark called Fort McHenry, where supposedly the national anthem was written. We enjoyed our time there and for a while it helped us forget our troubles. The next day we thanked the family for their hospitality, and continued the trip to our new home, Miami.

Chapter 4

MIAMI, MY NEW HOME

After we arrived, we stayed with some relatives for a few days until we got settled. I quickly noticed the difference in climate. In the daytime it was so hot and humid, that if you stayed too long in the sun it felt like you were melting away in the heat. The nights were not much better. Even with the windows open and the fans on, sometimes it became unbearable. My mother's health however, seemed to take a turn for the better.

My brother quickly found a job and my dad soon followed. We found this rental house next to some old friends from Cuba we had known all our lives. It was not a large house like the one that burned down, but it was all right. It was located in a convenient area, close to little Havana and many other places. We managed to live there for several years until my brother got married.

I began attending Miami Senior High School in the summer of 1967. I had to walk several blocks every day to Flagler St. to catch the bus to and from the school, and I quickly made some friends. One of them Victor, went on to become my best friend and later was my roommate when I attended the University of Florida in 1972. In the spring of 1970, I graduated from High School and quickly began to make preparations to attend college.

One of the things I really enjoyed about Miami was the beautiful beaches that it had. My brother and I tried to go every weekend and spend a lot of time snorkeling. Back then the reefs were still intact, and sea life was abundant. We used to spend hours just watching the variety in the color of the fishes there, and the different species. They were all different and beautiful: blue, yellow, orange, green, red, black and a mixture of all of the above.

Years later, the government started to dredge the beaches, and the oil tankers began to pollute the waters and kill most of the reefs and sea life. This eventually brought an end to our snorkeling expeditions. My brother had bought a 1965 Volkswagen, so he let my father keep the 1963 Buick. During this time my cousin whom I had affectionately nicknamed Mingo, my brother and I formed a band and began to play at private parties.

My brother played the base, my cousin the lead guitar and I would play the rhythm guitar and sing. We began to go everywhere and had a lot of fun together. My brother and I went to his house almost every evening to practice, especially on the weekends. However after a while, my brother met a girl who had just moved to Miami from up north, and he fell madly in love with her.

Soon after in the summer of 1970, they got married in St. Michaels Catholic Church. I was my brother's best man, and his fiancée's little sister was the flower girl. The wedding was really beautiful and Father Paniagua, our old parochial priest, performed the ceremony. Everyone celebrated their union in marriage, and wished them well. With less money coming in, after the wedding we were forced to move to a one bedroom apartment nearby.

The apartment was air conditioned and in a nicer area, but it was also much smaller. I got myself a job in the summer, and with the money I made bought a 1961 VW for $500. With the help of a government loan, I began attending Miami Dade Jr. College where I continued for two years and graduated with an Associate of Arts degree in 1972. All the time I attended College I kept working a part time job at the Winn Dixie meat department.

Because I had gotten a score of 714 on my SAT test, I was given a scholarship to the Univ. of Florida School of Electrical Engineering. I decided to take advantage of this opportunity and went to Gainesville with my old friend Victor. The very first impression I got when we arrived there was that the University was like a small city. There were about thirty thousand students in the school from all over the country, and some other parts of the world.

There was not much to do there, so we spent most of the time studying. In the weekends sometimes we played tennis or hung around the activities center where most of the students were playing in the game room or watching a movie in the theater. By the end of the school year, I had taken some courses in the field of Environmental Engineering, and I enjoyed it so much that I decided I was going to switch majors the first chance I got.

When I came home for the summer of 73, I found out that Florida International University had recently opened in the city of Miami, and was offering degrees in the field of Environmental Engineering. After visiting them and sitting down with a counselor, I came to the decision that I was going to finish my career there. That would help me save some money, plus I would be close to my family.

I put forth a great effort to take as many courses as I possibly could, and finish all the requirements to graduate with a Bachelor's Degree in Environmental Engineering by the end of that same school year. However, by the time I graduated in 74, Jimmy Carter had become president and the country was in a deep recession. That combined with the fact that I had just graduated and had no experience, made it extremely difficult to find a job in engineering.

In Search of a Job

I prepared a resume, and began filling applications in every engineering company in the area, but there were very few job openings. The ones that did have an opening were asking for some job experience which I did not have. It became the proverbial Catch 22; I could not get a job without experience, and I needed to have a job to get experience It was extremely frustrating.

A woman who lived next door to us informed me that a position for salesman of CB radios had just opened up in the company where she worked, and if I was interested she would talk to the president. Having no other options and the economy looking quite bleak, I decided to take her up on the offer and started working there. The pay was not that great, but the job was very easy and there was not really any pressure.

On the spring of 75, my uncle offered me a job in a construction company owned by his son. He told me that although it was not a position as an engineer, it would be a good opportunity for me to learn about construction and thus get me started on the right track. I would be working on the site of a new construction project in the city of Goulds, about an hour's drive from where we lived.

I resigned my position as a CB salesman, and thanked our lady friend for giving me the opportunity. After a few days I started working at the new job. The pay was not much better, and the hours were much longer. Since I had to be at the job by 7 am, I had to leave home by at least 6 am every day. My boss was demanding and had zero tolerance for error. I began to get the feeling that I had made a huge mistake, as I would soon find out.

The construction project was in a black neighborhood, so the black men who lived in the area began to demand that they be hired for construction work. Slowly they began doing small peaceful demonstrations in front of the project carrying signs and protesting, but as the days passed I began to notice that they were becoming increasingly hostile. I tried to warn the owners that the situation might get worse, but they did not listen.

One day when I got to my job, they had blocked the entrance and were standing in front of it with clubs and knives. When I tried to go in through the gate, they began to make threatening moves as if they were going to bust the windshield of my car with their clubs. Having only minimal liability insurance on my car and no money to fix it, I was not about to let these men destroy my car which was the only means of getting to my job.

I went to a phone booth nearby and called my job explaining the situation. I was not prepared to hear what they said on the other end. I was told that it was my duty to report to work no matter what the situation, and that if I did not, I would loose my job. I felt like telling them to shove it, but I managed to exercise great self control and hung up without saying a word. I got in my car and drove home, knowing I was without a job again.

When I told my parents what happened, they became incensed and really let my uncle have it. After a few days they called be back to apologize, and offered me another position, but I knew better. I was not about to play the fool twice in a row. I had learned my lesson. I went back to my old job at the Winn Dixie meat department where I worked for the next several months. It was closer, same pay, better hours and I did not have to take all the hassle.

I had applied for a job at Wingerter Laboratories as a Lab Technician several months before, and had been told that if a position became available, they would call me. After months of working for Winn Dixie, they offered to send me to school to train me as a butcher, but I declined. I decided to wait for a better position to open in my field of expertise. Meanwhile, I became a U.S. citizen and was now qualified to vote in all future elections.

A few weeks later I received a call from Wingerter Laboratories telling me that a position as Lab Technician had just become available, and asked me if I was still interested. Quickly I answered with a resounding YES. I then gave a few days notice to Winn Dixie, and began to work at my new job. I worked at Wingerter Laboratories for two years, and during that time I purchased my first new car, a 1976 red Dodge Aspen.

There was only one more person working with me in the

laboratory, his name was Enrique. He was an older Cuban man who had worked there for several years. He had a lot of experience and was instrumental in my success during my time at Wingerter Labs. He taught me a lot about laboratory techniques and all the chemical procedures. I learned a lot from him as he was very meticulous and precise in his work.

My time working at Wingerter Labs was peaceful, and it helped me to heal from a turbulent relationship I had just come out of. I would often have go out on the field to collect water samples, and then bring them to the lab for testing. We tested the samples for Biochemical Oxygen Demand (BOD), Chemical Oxygen Demand (COD), Iron, Fluoride, and all kinds of trace elements. We would even conduct tests on all kinds of petroleum products.

One day while hanging out in the fall of 77, my cousin mentioned to me that he had a good friend who had just been made the president of Deltona, a developer of small communities in South Florida. I asked him to speak to his friend on my behalf, and try to help me land a job there. After a few days, he gave me his friend's phone number for me to call him. When I spoke to him, he quickly asked me to come in the following week for an interview.

The interview went great, and before the day was over I was offered a job as a Sanitary Engineer working in their Utilities Department. Although I really enjoyed my work at Wingerter Labs, I could not pass this opportunity. I was going to be working for a well known and respected company as an Engineer, making more money and much closer to home. This is the kind of stuff that dreams are made out of. Finally I had landed my dream job.

The Utilities Department consisted of four draftsmen, two engineers, a supervisor and the chief department engineer plus the secretary. The supervisor was a good engineer, but he was very tough on us. It was extremely difficult to drag information out of him, and when he did finally share it with you, it was the minimal for you to be able to do your work. It was very frustrating trying to do your work and not have the information to do it.

Whenever I went to him to ask him some questions, he would say: "I don't want questions, I want answers". He drove the guys there really hard, almost ruthlessly. It was an exasperating situation to say the least. At times I thought of quitting, but I really needed this job; and perhaps more importantly, I needed the experience that I was getting there. So I decided I would humble myself, and put up with it for a season.

In the meantime, my brother had lost his job and now he had a child. He had been very good to us in the past, and now I was in a position to help him out. I quickly got him a job at Deltona's accounting department that turned out to be really good for him. Sometimes we went home together for lunch at my mother's, and we got to spend the most time together since he had gotten married. We talked about work, old times and life in general.

By the time 1979 arrived, I had been at the company a couple of years and the economy had gotten better. I began to look in the Sunday classified ads for engineering job openings, and after a few months I found an ad from Greenleaf and Telesca looking for Civil Engineers. After an interview they offered me a position in the Engineering Department, with great benefits and a better salary.

I began working for them right away, and eventually was even given my very own office. The company treated their employees well, and I really enjoyed my time working there. I had a good boss who taught a lot about the business, and answered all the questions I had without giving me a hassle. He was a quiet and humble man who treated his employees with dignity and respect.

During this time, however I had gotten romantically involved with another girl. At first things were going fine, but after a couple of years I discovered that I was not ready for marriage. The breakup left a terrible taste in my mouth, and a deep scar in my heart. I promised myself that I would never get married. Then I began drinking excessively, to the point where I carried a bottle of whiskey under the seat of my car at all times.

I tried to go to Catholic Mass occasionally, and took confession and communion once in a while, but somehow something was missing. A friend of mine at work seeing my condition, tried to help me out and invited me to attend a Catholic Charismatic retreat called "De Colores", which I attended hoping that it would help. I enjoyed the energy, the faith and the slight presence of God's Spirit that I felt there. I left hungry for His Holy Spirit.

A few days later, I asked for an appointment to speak to our parochial priest, Paniagua. We had in past times had some deep theological discussions, but he was not prepared for what I was about to ask him. When we met, I asked him point blank about the Holy Spirit, and how to be filled with Him. To my astonishment, the little priest proceeded to tell me to forget about the experience, that it was not a good thing to be involved in such fanaticism.

You can well imagine my total disappointment. Just when I thought I had found what I was looking for, man and religion got in the way. I began to explain to him how empty I felt, and that no matter how many times I went to confession and communion, I kept committing the same sins again and again. When he said to just keep coming to Mass on Sundays and forget my experience, I told him that I was not a hypocrite, and would not return.

The Wasted Years

That started a period of time in my life where I began living a worldly, crazy lifestyle. A friend of mine at work, who had just gone to study medicine at Santo Domingo, left his furnished bachelor's pad to me for a very decent monthly rental, only with the condition that he could use it when he came home during the holidays. This was an offer that there was no way I could turn down.

I moved into the new place, and I really began to live it up. I really was not a bad person, but I started hanging around with the wrong crowd. Every weekend, my friends and I would go out to the night clubs to party and we would sniff some coke, smoke grass and then hit the bottle. No matter what, we always managed to end up getting drunk and sleeping around with girls.

I still loved God, but I wanted nothing to do with any type of organized religion. I had tried almost all of them: Baptist, Methodist, Episcopal, Presbyterian, Catholic, Jehovah's Witnesses, and none of them had what I was looking for. I just wanted the awesome presence of God, the precious Holy Spirit, but all I ever found in these places was a lot of religion and man.

Oh yes, they would all read the Bible, and preach their sermons. But even the precious word of God without the anointing of the Holy Spirit, is dead. I once thought that all preaching was good no matter who does the preaching or what is being preached. But that is not so; without the infilling of the Holy Spirit, we are dead. Dead men preach dead sermons, and dead sermons will kill you spiritually.

The apostle Paul said it best in 2 Corinthians 3:6 "...for the letter kills, but the spirit gives life." If you don't have the word of God preached to you by an anointed vessel, it will slowly kill you spiritually. You see, we all are spirit beings, who have a soul and live in a physical body. As spiritual beings, the only thing that we can feed on is the living word of God. The word of God without the anointing of the Spirit is just logos, not rhema (alive).

That is the reason why you have many false religions and sects who read the Bible every day and yet, they are dead spiritually. The Scribes, Pharisees and Sadducees read the scriptures every day for hours, and yet when the Messiah came, they were not able to recognize Him. It takes the precious Holy Spirit to anoint the word of God and make it alive (rhema) to us, otherwise it will just be dead letters that can kill you.

The Bible is not just another book, it is a supernatural book. It can be read by everyone and enjoyed as a good book, but it can only be understood under the anointing of the Holy Spirit. When the word of God goes through a vessel that is filled and anointed by the Holy Spirit, it becomes alive; and when you hear the word preached, it will speak, minister and impart life unto your spirit man.

When young people do not get exposed to the real supernatural presence and power of God, they begin to look for the Him in the wrong places. This is exactly what happened to me; eventually I started to look for Papa God by reading occult books from Ouspensky, Castañeda, Gurdjieff and others. I spent several years on this quest, while I kept living "la vida loca" (the crazy lifestyle). But all the time, the Lord Jesus had his hand on my life.

Then during one those weekends in the fall of 1980, I went partying with my friends to a club called The Alley Cat, and that was where I met my present day wife, Yvette. She was sitting at a table, seemingly lost in her thoughts. I approached her and asked her if she wanted to have a drink with me and dance. To my surprise, she turned me down. But then, when I asked her if I could sit down with her at the table and just talk, she said yes.

We talked all night, and I found out that she had just had an experience with Jesus Christ that had touched her deeply. Although I did not understand it, I was not very interested in hearing about it. Religion had left a real bad taste in my mouth. Nevertheless, we started going out, and for the next several months we saw each other every weekend. I liked being with her, but all she could talk to me about was her experience with Jesus.

Eventually, she asked me to go with her to the church where she had this wonderful experience she kept telling me about, and though I was not too keen on the idea, I indulged her. When we got there, she introduced me to all these people who seemed to be genuinely happy and friendly, and then we sat in one of the pews towards the back of the church. At first, everything went pretty much the same as the other churches I had been to before.

However, when the people started to worship God, I began to feel something very strange. It was as though something or someone (as I found out later), was trying to get inside of me. I began to feel uncomfortable and told her that I really wanted to leave. She left reluctantly, and the asked me to begin attending church with her on a regular basis. This was more than I had bargained for, and I was not about to get involved with religion again.

As we continued to go out together, I noticed that she would not have drinks with me, did not want to sleep with me, and had this habit of talking about Jesus all the time. When I finally had enough of that, I told her that our relationship was not going to work, and that it would be better if we just ended the relationship and each went our own way. It seemed to me that we were like two ships going in totally different directions. Boy was I wrong.

I had money, girls, and a beautiful bachelor's pad all to myself and yet, I still had this empty feeling in my gut that could not be filled with any of these things. It was as if the more I tried to fill my emptiness with all these things, the worse the emptiness became. Sometimes I wondered if this was everything that there was to life, and what part did God play in all of this, if there even was a God at all. I began to have serious doubts.

I now know that Yvette and many other people were praying for me all this time that I would open my heart to Jesus and let Him in. But I was not ready yet. God had to allow me to hit rock bottom before He could rescue me. Just like someone who is drowning in the sea, you cannot attempt to rescue him until he begins to drown. And I was not drowning just yet. I was about to experience the depths of despair and loneliness.

It is really interesting how quickly the Lord can turn your life around when the appointed time has arrived. Just like a fish caught on a hook by an expert fisherman, no matter how much he fights and tries to swim away, he begins to be reeled in slowly, until he winds up in the boat in the hands of the fisherman. That is exactly how it felt when I began to be reeled in by the Lord. No matter how much I fought it, the feeling would just not go away.

Through the years, my friend Sergio and I had never had any problems. We had a good friendship and knew how to stay out of each other's way. Then one day we got into a really stupid argument, and stopped going out drinking for a while. He had been my drinking buddy for years, and now I had no one to hang around with. One Friday night he called me to ask if I wanted to go out and hit the clubs with him; but I was so tired of the same routine that I told him I was going to stay home. I was not ready however, for the experience I would have next.

Chapter 5

THE CALLING

I stayed home that night all by myself, and had a talk with God in my own simple way. I told Him that I was tired and fed up with my life, and that if He really existed, I needed Him to speak to me and help me out. I really poured out my heart to God that night, in the hopes that somehow He would be able to hear me. Little did I realize that was the opening He had been waiting for, and later that night I had an encounter that I will never forget.

I was sound sleep when I was abruptly awakened by several knocks on the door and someone softly calling my name. I quickly looked at my wrist watch and noticed it was 1 am. The first thought through my head was that it was my friend Sergio who had come to get me to go partying and was knocking on the door calling my name. I put some clothes on and opened the door expecting to find him there, but to my surprise there was no one.

I looked everywhere, but there was no sign of anyone. As I closed the door and went back to bed, I had this sense of foreboding come all over me. It began to dawn on me that the one doing the knocking and calling my name was not someone from this world. I took this huge catholic bible that was lying on top of a table just for looks (because I never read it) and put it on my bed.

So I told God that if it was him that had knocked on the door and called out my name, to please speak to me through it when I opened the Bible at random. As I laid hold of the bible and opened it at random, my eyes came to rest on a verse from the book of John 3:3: "...Verily, verily, I say unto you, except a man be born again, he cannot see the kingdom of God." Suddenly I realized that I was experiencing an epiphany, a personal God moment.

However, being the stubborn man that I am, I wanted more proof. Again I asked God to speak to me when I opened up my big bible at random, and it opened to the book of Revelation 3:20: "Behold, I stand at the door and knock. If anyone hears my voice and opens the door, then I will come in to him, and will dine with him, and he with me." It became increasingly obvious to me that God Himself was speaking to me personally.

I was almost persuaded, just not quite yet. Brother, you talk about a doubting Thomas, I was it. So I told God to please not be upset with me, that I really needed Him to talk to me one more time through the Bible just to be sure this was real, and not some bizarre coincidence. As I placed the big bible on my bed, it fell open to the book of Revelation 22:7 "Behold, I come quickly: blessed is he that keeps the sayings of the prophecy of this book."

I closed the Bible and just sat in my chair, drinking in everything that had taken place that night. The Lord was telling me in no uncertain terms that He was knocking on the door of my heart, telling me that I needed to be born again because He was coming back soon. I sensed a very strong presence of God in my pad that night. In the past, I had felt His presence ever since I was a child, but I had never experienced anything like this.

That same night I had a vision of the night. I was in this room with many people dressed in white. They all seemed to be paying attention to one man that was lying on his back on a bed, and there was someone performing what seemed to be some complicated open heart surgery on him. As I moved closer to take a better look, a man dressed in white, who I now realize was an angel, walked towards me and motioned for me to get closer.

I told him no, as I quickly turned around and ran out of the room. At that moment I woke up and thought it had been just a dream. But that was not the end of that. A couple of days later, I dreamt that I was in the same place with the same people, but this time the same angel took me by the arm, and no matter what I did or say, I was not able to resist the force that was pushing me closer and closer to a very mysterious door.

The angel quickly led me to the open door and gently pushed me through it. I knew I had no choice but to walk through it. However, I was not prepared for what I was about to see as I made my way to the other side.

A Visit to Heaven

As I stepped through the door I saw the most beautiful place I have ever seen in my life. Throughout my life, I have been to some of the most beautiful places in this country, and other parts of the world. I have been to the highest mountain peaks in Yosemite, California; the Catskill Mountains in New York; the Blue Ridge Mountains of Tennessee, as well as other beautiful places in Spain, Honduras, Mexico, Cuba, Nicaragua and Puerto Rico.

But everything about this place was otherworldly; it was full of light, life, love and music. The colors which I saw there were so rich and vivid, the kind of colors I had never seen before. The grass I saw was so green and full of life; the sky above me was a kind of deep blue, almost translucent. Everything there seemed to be vibrating with live and intricately connected to each other. The best way to put it is that everything was completely perfect.

The flowers, trees, grass, everything seemed to be radiating life, love, music as well as a feeling of well being that made me feel connected, and a part of it. Then I saw the most beautiful tree planted in the center of this place. It caught my attention because of the radiance, life and energy that seemed to emanate from it. As I began to approach the tree, I noticed that there was a scroll in one of the branches, almost beckoning me to take it.

I proceeded to take the scroll from the branch of this extraordinary tree, when I noticed that it contained some strange writings all over it. Somehow, I instinctively knew that the scroll was a part of the tree, almost like a fruit, and that the contents of the writings in the scroll were extremely important. However, I was so enthralled by the beauty of everything around me, and the excitement of what was taking place that I neglected to read the scroll.

There was so much to see that I continued to walk; surely, I could always read the scroll later on. But then suddenly, the same man who had brought me in grabbed me by the arm and pulled me out of that wonderful place. He then proceeded to take the scroll from my hand and told me that I was not ready to continue my journey there. When I asked him why, he simply said: "You have not even read the scroll". Then I abruptly woke up.

I spent the next several weeks thinking about and meditating on the strange events of that night. I kept it close to my heart and did not share it with anyone, who would believe me anyway? Then one day out of the blue Yvette, my present day wife, called me at work to talk to me. She began to tell me some weird excuse for calling me, but frankly I did not care. I knew that somehow God was involved and I felt like seeing her again anyway.

We started dating again for several months and she started taking me to church with her again. I still felt very strange whenever I went to that Pentecostal Church with her, but because of the experience I had, I was now more open to everything. Then one day after service, Yvette introduced me to this red haired man named Art Snitzer who was the head of the Church's Home Bible Studies.

He quickly offered to teach me a home bible study if I would commit to meeting with him in my place once a week for one hour, for about twelve weeks. That did not seem like a bad deal, and besides that was the only way Yvette would continue to go out with me. As we went through the first few lessons, it was really boring. He was a really good teacher, but all the stories of Abraham, Noah, and Moses I had already heard before.

I had begun to think that the bible study was really a waste of time when he started to teach me the lesson on the tabernacle. Suddenly, I became very interested in the types and shadows contained in the tabernacle plan representing God's plan of redemption for mankind. From that point on, he had my attention. The deeper we went into the plan of salvation, the clearer things began to get for me. Everything Jesus said started to make sense...

"...I am the way, the truth, and the life: no man comes unto the Father, but by me." John 14:6

"I am the door: if any one enters in by me, he shall be saved, and shall go in and shall go out and shall find pasture." John 10:7-9

"But you shall receive power, after the Holy Spirit has come upon you: and you shall be witnesses unto me both in Jerusalem, and in all Judea, and in Samaria, and unto the uttermost part of the earth." Acts 1:8

Other scriptures in the Bible made sense as well...

"I will give you a new heart, and I will put a new spirit within you; I will take away the stony heart out of your flesh, and I will give you a heart of flesh." Ezekiel 36:26

"But he is a Jew who is one inwardly; and circumcision is that of the heart, in the spirit not in the letter; whose praise is not of men, but of God." Romans 2:29

"Being made manifest that ye are an epistle of Christ, ministered by us, written not with ink, but with the Spirit of the living God; not in tables of stone, but in tables that are hearts of flesh." 2 Corinthians 3:3

"He that hath an ear let him hear what the Spirit says to the churches. To him that overcomes, to him will I give to eat of the tree of life, which is in the Paradise of God." Revelation 2:7

"Blessed are they that wash their robes, that they may have the right to come to the tree of life, and may enter in by the gates into the city." Revelation 22:14

"And I went unto the angel, and said unto him, Give me the little scroll. And he said unto me, Take it, and eat it up; and it shall make your stomach bitter, but it shall be in your mouth sweet as honey. And I took the little scroll out of the angel's hand, and ate it up; and it was in my mouth sweet as honey: and as soon as I had eaten it, my stomach was bitter. And he said unto me, you must prophesy again about many peoples, and nations, and tongues, and kings." Revelation 10:9-11

Slowly I began to understand what had happened to me, and the full meaning behind all of the things that I was shown during my visit to that wonderful place (which I now understand was heaven) on that fateful night in my bachelor's pad. Whether it was a vision of the night or I was literally taken there, I do not know. All I know is that what happened to me on that night literally impacted my life forever, and prepared me for what was to come next.

My Conversion

As I continued to go to church with Yvette, one Sunday evening during service, she took me to the altar with her and several men began to lay hands on me and pray for me. One of them began to rebuke evil spirits in me which I found to be very odd. Another man began telling me to worship God from my heart which I sincerely tried to do. All of a sudden, I began to scream at the top of my lungs for no reason at all. Things just kept getting weirder.

The screams were coming from deep within me. After I stopped screaming, I asked one of the men praying for me if I had screamed, to which he answered no. I then asked someone else if I had screamed; again the answer was no. I could not understand what had happened to me until much later on in my life. Without realizing it, I had received deliverance from evil spirits. As they were leaving me, they left screaming with a loud voice.

This is mentioned in Acts 8:7: "For unclean spirits came out of many of those who had them. They came out, crying with a loud voice." I felt better afterwards but a bit strange. A battle began raging between the kingdom of darkness and the kingdom of light for my soul. You see, evil spirits do not give up that easy whenever they have control of someone and they are kicked out. The Bible speaks about this quite a bit...

"When the unclean spirit is gone out of a man, he walks through dry places, seeking rest; and finding none, he says, I will return unto my house from which I came out." Luke 11:24

Some time later as I was sleeping on my bed alone at night, I heard this strange loud rattling noise that woke me up. As I sat up in my bed, I said out loud: "who is there", and I heard this raspy voice answer: "I am thirsty". I quickly discerned it was a demon that was harassing me, so I rebuked the evil spirit in the name of Jesus and commanded him to leave and never come back to bother me. He never came back to harass me.

As I continued to take the home bible study, the Lord began to deal with me in a very special way that it was time to make a decision. I know that Yvette was praying for me, as well as a slew of saints in the church. One day after hearing a message on salvation, Yvette asked me if I wanted to give my heart to the Lord and make Him my Lord and Savior. I nodded, and she quickly led me in a prayer of repentance to receive Jesus into my heart.

I felt much better after that, as if a weight had been lifted off my shoulders. However, I had this big empty feeling deep inside of me, and I knew that there was something more that I still needed in my life. One day I was having my home bible study and the lesson that night was on the baptism of the Holy Spirit. The more I heard about it, the more I grew convinced that the Holy Spirit is what I had been searching for all of my life.

Now I was being told and shown by scripture that this experience was available to me, today if I so wanted it. I immediately told Art that I wanted the baptism of the Holy Spirit and that I also wanted to be baptized in water. He informed me that the pastor was out of town but that he would be back on Wednesday. I asked him to set it up for that Wednesday. I became so excited that I could barely wait for that day to arrive.

My Baptism and Regeneration

When the anticipated Wednesday night finally arrived, Yvette and I arrived at the church early and went to see Pastor Rooks right away. To my surprise, he asked me if I would mind being baptized on Sunday instead. He gave me several reasons as to why it would be so much better: "the water in the baptismal tank was too cold"; "the water had not been changed in a while"; "there would be more people present on Sunday at church", and so on.

Well, like I said before I am a very stubborn man and I had made up my mind that I was going to be baptized on that night. Pastor Rooks finally realized he was not going to persuade me, so he asked Art to prep me for baptism. Jimmy, a big mentally challenged young man, went to the baptismal tank and performed his familiar trademark stirring of the waters ceremony with a big paddle that let everyone know that a water baptism was imminent.

I had to take off my clothes and put on a white robe in preparation for the baptism. Art was smiling and praying in tongues as well as Larry Fleming, his father in law who had come alongside to assist me. As I made my way up the stairs to the baptismal tank, a feeling of excitement suddenly came over me. I was about to experience the new birth experience. Scriptures from the Bible began to flood my mind at lightning speed:

"And I will pray the Father, and he shall give you another Comforter, that he may abide with you forever; Even the Spirit of truth; whom the world cannot receive, because it sees him not, neither knows him: but you know him; for he dwells with you, and shall be in you. I will not leave you comfortless: I will come to you." John 14:16-18

"For John truly baptized with water; but you shall be baptized with the Holy Spirit not many days from now. But you shall receive power, after the Holy Spirit has come upon you: and you shall be witnesses unto me both in Jerusalem, and in all Judea, and in Samaria, and unto the uttermost part of the earth." Acts 1:5, 8

"Then Peter said unto them, repent, and be baptized every one of you in the name of Jesus Christ for the remission of sins, and you shall receive the gift of the Holy Spirit. For the promise is unto you, and to your children, and to all that are afar off, even as many as the Lord our God shall call." Acts 2:38-39

As soon as I stepped into the baptismal tank and my feet touched the cold water, the power of God began to surge through my body. Once I was inside the tank, Pastor Rooks positioned my hands for baptism by having me hold my nose with my right hand, and my right wrist with my left hand. At that point he proceeded to ask me if I believed that Jesus had died for my sins, resurrected on the third day and ascended up to heaven.

When I answered yes, he said: "upon the confession of your faith, I now baptize you in the name of Jesus Christ for the remission of your sins" and put me under the waters in the baptismal tank. When I came out of the waters, he told me to worship God and He would fill me with the Holy Spirit. The moment I opened my mouth to worship the Lord, I began to stammer and then I heard

Pastor Rooks say: "that's it, that's it, keep going".

Then suddenly, I began to speak in a language I had never spoken before. As I was speaking in tongues, I could hear Art in the background saying: "Drink as much as you like Augusto; He is filling you with the Holy Spirit". I don't know how long I was there speaking in tongues; all I know is that I was experiencing emotions and things that cannot possibly be explained in earthly terms. I felt like waves of glory and love were going through me.

I had definitely never experienced anything like this in my entire life. How can something this wonderful not be preached from the pulpit of every church. No amount of biblical knowledge or religious activity could provide the God experience that I had received. In the past I had gone to many catholic masses, retreats and many kinds of evangelical churches seeking God, but the only thing I had ever found was religion.

We are all born spiritually dead into this world; we just don't know it. Our human spirit without the Spirit of God is dead, and the only way to really know God is through the new birth experience. It has nothing to do with being decent people, living clean moral lives or doing good, kind deeds. This is pleasing to God but has nothing to do with the new birth experience. This is exactly what Jesus told Nicodemus when he came to Him:

"Jesus answered and said unto him, Verily, verily, I say unto you, except a man be born again, he cannot see the kingdom of God. Nicodemus said unto him, how can a man be born when he is old? Can he enter the second time into his mother's womb, and be born? Jesus answered: Verily, verily, I say unto you, except a man be born of water and of the Spirit, he cannot enter into the

For days I felt like I was walking in a cloud. Everything looked so beautiful; the grass looked so green, the sky so blue, the colors so vivid. It seemed as though a dark veil that had been over my eyes all of my life had now been suddenly removed. I loved everyone, and wanted to tell them about Jesus. I felt the presence of the Holy Spirit so strong with me always, no matter where I was. I did not feel alone anymore; I had a constant companion.

I tried to speak in tongues everyday as much as I could, no matter where I was. The Lord became more real to me than my own family. When I read the Bible I could now understand it clearly and it was really exciting; not like before when it was boring because I did not understand it. I developed an insatiable hunger to learn everything there was to learn about the Bible, and read every Christian book I could lay my hands on.

I would pray every chance I got, and would not miss a single meeting at the church. We lived about thirty minutes away from the church, but for us it was a pleasure to go there every time the doors were open. I volunteered to do anything that needed to be done from cleaning toilets, mowing the grass, painting the walls to teaching home bible studies. It was a privilege to be able to serve my God and I did it with great pleasure.

I began to memorize verses of scriptures daily and do word studies, as well as witness to people about Jesus and His wonderful gift of the Holy Spirit. Soon Yvette and I enrolled in a three year Bible School program that was offered right at the church, and we could barely wait. I had never felt anything like what I had experienced, and I knew that I would never be the same again. Finally I found what I had been looking for all of my life.

My mother and father could not understand what I was feeling, even though I tried to explain it to them several times in many different ways. My friends frowned on me whenever I tried to tell them what I had experienced, and tried to make me believe that it would all pass away after a while. They began to treat me as though I had become some type of crazy fanatic, and I noticed that they would change the conversation whenever I got close to them.

However, I was not concerned with what they said or thought about me anymore. I had just had an experience and fallen madly in love with the most wonderful being I had ever met in my life, Jesus Christ. I had just found the pearl of great price, and I was not about to loose it or let anybody take it away from me:

"Again, the kingdom of heaven is like unto a merchant man, seeking goodly pearls: Who, when he had found one pearl of great price, went and sold all that he had, and bought it." Matthew 13:45-46

Chapter 6

THE BACHELOR GETS MARRIED

I asked Yvette to marry me shortly after I received the baptism of the Holy Spirit on October 7, 1981 and we set a date for the wedding on February 27 of the following year. This was a major miracle for me since I had made up my mind that I was going to remain a bachelor until I was at least forty years old. However, the Lord had other plans for my life as we shall see later on.

We began to make plans for the wedding right away, as we barely had four months to take care of everything. Our church really helped us a lot with the wedding preparations, and did not charge us a cent for anything. That came in quite handy as I had used all the savings I had to buy new furniture for our new home, and pay for the rent, electricity and gas deposits.

My father was the manager of an apartment building complex, a position that I had helped him secure with the owner of the building a few years before. The building had eight apartments, and my parents lived in apartment number one in the first floor. All the apartments were taken except one two doors down from where my parents lived. I immediately rented it in hopes that my mother would teach Yvette how to cook Cuban cuisine.

I moved into our new furnished apartment and allowed Yvette to move into my bachelor's pad. She had recently lost her job and was not able to pay the rent for the place she was living in. Doing things this way was more difficult and expensive for me, but I did not want her name to be tainted by having her move in with me, especially living so close to my parents; I respected them too much.

I never raised my voice to them, let alone talk back to them. I do not understand how in today's modern society people disrespect and dishonor their parents without even thinking about it twice. This has nothing to do with who is right or wrong, and everything to do with respecting and honoring someone so much that you do not want to do or say anything that will hurt them, offend them or take away their dignity; even to defend yourself.

"This know also, that in the last days perilous times shall come. For men shall be lovers of their own selves, covetous, boasters, proud, blasphemers, disobedient to parents, unthankful, unholy, without natural affection, covenant breakers, false accusers, incontinent, fierce, despisers of those that are good, traitors, reckless, conceited, lovers of pleasures more than lovers of God." 2 Timothy 3:1-4

At the beginning of 1982 the U.S. economy began to get sluggish, and most companies began to lay off people to be able to survive. A month right before the wedding,I was laid off from my engineering job. I had worked for this company for three years, and was really counting on this job to pay all the bills that were mounting daily. This was my very first test as a Christian, and one that I had determined I was not going to fail.

I started looking for a job right away. I would buy the Sunday papers, and look in the classifieds section for an open position in the area of civil engineering. I would call one company after another trying to get an appointment for a job interview, and went to many. But in every case I was told that they were not hiring at all right now, but that they would keep my resume and application in file.

Everybody began to give me advice on what to do, and everyone was telling me to postpone the wedding until I had found a job. However, the plans were made and the expenses for the wedding had been incurred, so any kind of postponement was out of the question. When I finally told everybody that I was getting married on the planned date regardless of whether I had a job or not, I was then told by the same people to postpone the honeymoon trip.

You only have one real honeymoon in marriage, so I decided I needed to have a heart to heart talk with my heavenly Papa. I went to my prayer closet and told the Lord how bad I really needed Him to help me. I basically told Him that I was His child; that I belonged to Him and the problem I had was really His. I do not know where I got the boldness to come up with that prayer; but I did.

I had determined that we were not only going to go ahead and get married, but we were going to go on our honeymoon as if everything was alright. After all, it was now in the capable hands of my heavenly father. I do not know where that faith came from, but it was supernatural the way it just manifested in me. I had the certainty, the assurance that when we returned from the honeymoon, I would have a job waiting for me. I just knew that I knew.

The Wedding

Our wedding was simple, but at the same time it was beautiful. All our family was there along with the distant relatives and friends that came to share our special moment of happiness. Needless to say, my parents were very happy that their bachelor son was finally settling down and getting married. My brother, who was a good photographer, took all the pictures in our wedding and gave it to us as a wedding present.

All our family, knowing about our financial situation, gave us money as a wedding gift so we would be able to go on our honeymoon. Even so, we did not have enough to go on a cruise, take a plane to Cancun or anything like that. So we decided we would travel in my 81 Honda Civic up the Florida east coast all the way to Jacksonville and return back home on the west coast, stopping at all the major attractions along the way.

I was not concerned about the future, nor did I allow my lack of a job to hinder me from having a good time with my wife during our honeymoon. I just knew in my heart that everything was going to be all right. I felt that God was with me in a very tangible way; I could feel His presence with us in the car throughout the whole trip. It was wonderful to experience the living God this way.

When we got back home, my dad was waiting for me outside and quickly came to me with a big smile on his face and told me some great news. He said that while I was gone, I had received a phone call from one of the engineering companies that had interviewed me, and they had a job opening for me. I was so happy, that I began to hug and kiss everybody. I had passed my first test and my heavenly father rewarded me with a miracle.

When I went to talk to the people in the company, I asked him how the position had become open, since I had been told just a few weeks before that there was no job opening. He told me, shrugging his shoulders, that on Friday (the same day I had my talk with the Lord) the man who had my position as Head of the Sanitary Engineering Department, had come into his office and unexpectedly resigned without offering any explanation.

We settled into our new apartment right away and I began in my new job the next day. I really liked my new job, my new boss, and the company was just a few minutes away from our home. Everything was going well for us. Yvette was learning how to cook Cuban food from my mother, and she was doing a lot of practicing on me. I did not mind putting up with hard black beans and the salty beef steak, as long as she was making progress.

Those first three years of my marriage were magical. Yvette and I would go on long trips during my two weeks vacation time. We went to San Francisco and visited China Town, and got to eat in one of their best Chinese restaurants. We traveled through the Golden Gate Bridge, and drove all the way to Yosemite Park, as we went up to Glacier Point as well as down to the Great Sequoia

Groves in the valley. We looked forward to these vacation times.

We would save money during the year so we could afford to go on these vacations. We understood the value of sacrifice, and knew that in order to have some things in life, you have to give up other things. We went to the Smokey Mountains, visited Arlington Cemetery; toured the Statue of Liberty in New York City and the museums in Washington DC. We went to Disney World so many times I lost count. These were the best of times for us.

We became very involved with the church, attending every service, every activity and volunteering to help with work anywhere that it was needed. We became involved with Art's Home Bible Study program and began teaching home bible studies to someone every week. In addition, we began teaching Sunday school to little children in a poor neighborhood every Saturday. Yvette would go get the children in their homes, while I prepared the lesson.

Later that same year we began attending Bible School in the church every Tuesday night. The curriculum was taught by Sister Herring, and a couple named Norman and Kathy Webster. They were all very good teachers, and made the classes really interesting. I loved attending the classes every week as it fueled my insatiable hunger for knowledge about the Bible, and kept our minds busy. I learned a lot about the Bible, and it built up my faith.

I had been given a wonderful private parking space in my new job, except that there was a tree right next to it that produced these obnoxious berries that left a stain when they fell on my car. I went to talk to my boss about the possibility of maybe changing my parking space as I explained my problem to him. He told me that was the only parking space available, but that if I did not want it, I could give it up and park a block away under the bridge.

I politely thanked him, and told him that I would keep my parking space regardless. I continued to deal with the berries falling on my car, as I had to wash my car just about everyday as I came home from work. This went on for several weeks, until one afternoon I was coming out of work and as I got to my car, it was completely covered with the blessed berries. A righteous indignation came all over me as I faced the tree and cursed it in Jesus name.

I got into my car, and drove home and forgot all about the incident. Next day as I got to work, I noticed the tree had lost all its leaves, and all the berries were on the floor as if a mighty hand had shaken it during the night. It had dried up somehow during the night, and I was completely shocked at the whole thing. I would have never thought that the tree was really going to dry up and die. Needless to say, I never had any more problems with the berries.

The Birthing of My Ministry

One day that same year, when we were coming out of the Sunday morning service, we met ex-missionaries to Colombia Lewis and Sally Morley, who had recently come from Texas and started a Spanish church next to the church we attended. When he saw me, he came over to me and said: "I want you to come and preach for us next Sunday morning". I quickly reminded him that I was not a preacher, and would not know what to do. He simply looked at me and repeated the same thing again: "Just come preach for us; share your testimony".

The Lord had laid a trap for me that I simply was not able to escape from. Next Sunday came and I preached my first message. It was a simple message of faith mixed in with my testimony. God confirmed the message that morning with His anointing and signs following, as one person was saved and everyone was blessed.

I continued to preach from that day on, with many other pastors inviting me to come and preach in their churches. It has been twenty eight years since then and I have not stopped preaching. I began to take notice that people received the baptism of the Holy Spirit very easily when I prayed for them. After some time, many people began receiving the Holy Ghost in the same service when I prayed for them. It was like I was born to do this.

I began to spend more time in prayer with the Lord as I was growing spiritually more and more each day. I got every book I could find on the gifts of the Holy Spirit and began to consume them, as well as any other material that others recommended to me. I read the biographies of John G. Lake, Praying Hide, Kathryn Kuhlman, as well as the chronicles of great revivals of the past like Azusa, the Great Awakening, the Welch Revival and others.

I spent a lot of time talking to my spiritual father and mentor Lewis Morley, picking his brain about many topics like prayer, fasting, revival, his personal experiences in his missions work in Colombia and whatever questions I had. He was always supportive of me and never too busy whenever I needed to talk to him. His encouragement helped me during difficult times, and his teachings and example to this day, serve as a guide in my own ministry.

In the Spring of 1985, as we were getting ready to graduate from Bible School I began to feel a burden to start a church in the Greater Miami area where my parents lived, since there was no full gospel church in that whole region. There were many traditional churches like Catholic, Baptist, Methodist, Presbyterian, Episcopal, Lutheran, even the Jehovah's Witnesses had a church. I had tried them all before, and did not find what I wanted.

There was only one problem; I could not start a church without a license and permission from the denomination I belonged to. This had to be done through my local pastor who had never given a license to anyone before. I went to pastor Rooks and shared with him my intentions about starting a church, and asked him for a license application. I could tell that it was going to be an uphill battle to say the least; however, I knew that I had to obey the Lord.

He reluctantly gave me the license application, which I quickly filled out and returned to him for his signature. I waited about a week, and then I decided to ask him about it. He told me that he had not forgotten about me, and that he would get around to it sometime. A week went by, two weeks, a month and nothing. People began to come to me like Job's friends with very negative reports, discouraging me even more than I was already.

I did not understand why he would not sign and return my license application. I had been faithful for over three years, attended all church services, paid my tithes, gave love offerings and done everything I was ever asked to do. My character was beyond reproach, and I was active winning people to the Lord through Home Bible Studies and personal evangelism. I had attended three years of Bible School and was now about to graduate with honors.

Eventually, my frustration began to show as I began to loose my joy and zeal of going to church services. Some people began to take notice and tried to encourage me. However, through their feeble efforts and righteous facade, I could discern a religious spirit operating whose real intention was only to mock me. These same religious spirits are operating today in the church, spouting the same self righteous, holier than thou garbage from hell.

Jesus wrestled with these spirits when He was on the earth. He preached the gospel to the poor and fed them, healed the sick, cleansed the lepers, raised the dead, cast out devils and they still call Him Beelzebub. The real issue that was eating at their hearts was envy and jealousy. They were unable to do the works that He did, but yet they refused to repent and humble themselves before the mighty hand of God as a little child.

It is all about money, power and control. It has always been the same throughout the history of mankind. If it does not help their finances, church, ministry or benefit them in some way, they are not remotely interested. This is arrogantly contrary to the kingdom principles taught by the Lord Jesus Christ Himself throughout the gospels, as reflected in the following scriptures:

"Then said Jesus unto his disciples, If any man will come after me, let him deny himself, and take up his cross, and follow me." Matthew 16:24

"Verily, verily, I say unto you, except a grain of wheat falls into the ground and dies, it abides alone: but if it dies, it brings forth much fruit." John 12:24

"And he said unto them: The kings of the Gentiles exercise lordship over them; and they that exercise authority upon them are called benefactors. But you shall not be so: but he that is greatest among you let him be as the younger; and he that is chief, as he that does serve." Luke 22:25-26

I knew this was my second test from God to see how I would handle the situation. I was tempted several times to go into the pastor's office and tell him in no uncertain terms: "take the application and s____ it" as I walked out of his church never to return, and started a new church in Miami, Florida without his blessing or approval. However, the Lord helped me to exercise self control, and I decided instead to humble myself and wait for God to move.

Faith That Can Move Mountains

One Sunday evening during service, the choir began to sing the song "Open the Gates Oh Jerusalem, and Let the King of Glory Come In". As they began to repeat the song over and over again, the Spirit of God came upon me and I began to travail with groaning, moaning, and sounds that I could barely utter. Jimmy, the big boy, was sitting right next to me along with my wife, and the Spirit of God jumped on them both as they began speaking in tongues.

Everyone knew that the Lord was in the house and He was trying to give a message, but the gifts of the Spirit were not allowed to operate in that church, as is the case today in most churches in America. Today the Church of Jesus Christ, the New Jerusalem, has shut the gates and is not allowing the King of Glory to come in and have His way. This is the tragic truth, and it grieves me to say it.

I decided that it was time to have a heart to heart talk with Papa. I told Him that there was a mountain in my path that I needed him to move. I told Him that I needed the pastor to sign the application and give it back to me as soon as possible; however, if that was not His will, I would be willing to sit down on the pew and be a good Christian. I was not going to rebel against the authority that the Lord had placed over my life.

It went against everything within me to act in such a way, and I knew that I would fail the test if I did. When I finished my conversation with Papa, I walked away with peace to accept His decision, no matter what it was. A few days went by, and the following Sunday as I was in the morning service worshipping God, I noticed that the pastor was not on the platform where he usually was during service. There was a shift in the atmosphere.

I knew something was going on in the spirit realm. As the worship service continued, out of nowhere Brother Fleming, an elder in the church, came to where I was sitting and said to me: "Pastor Rooks wants to see you in his office right now". With a frown on my face I looked at my wife, as I got up and followed Brother Fleming all the way to the Pastor's office. Sitting behind his desk with my signed application before him was Brother Rooks.

As I came in, he told me to pull a chair and sit down. He then pushed the signed application towards me and said: "There is your signed application for a ministerial license. Go and start that church God told you to." As he did, I could not believe what had just transpired. God had just performed another miracle just as big as the one He had performed with my job three years before. Everyone in the church could not believe what had just happened.

God is able to deal with the hearts of kings, presidents and give you favor with people in positions of authority just like He did with Daniel, Joseph and all the heroes of the faith in Hebrews 11. He is the same yesterday, today and forever. What He has done for others He will do for you too, but you must believe it. If you allow doubt to get into your heart, it will erode the foundation of your faith until you begin to doubt even the reality of God:

"For verily I say unto you, that whosoever shall say unto this mountain, be removed, and be cast into the sea; and shall not doubt in his heart, but shall believe that those things which he said shall come to pass; he shall have whatsoever he said. Therefore I say unto you, whatever things you desire, when you pray, believe that you will receive them, and you shall have them." Mark 11:23-24

"Jesus answered and said unto them, 'Verily I say unto you, if you have faith and doubt not, you shall not only do this which is done to the fig tree, but also if you shall say unto this mountain, be removed and be cast into the sea, it shall be done. And all things, whatsoever you shall ask in prayer believing, you shall receive." Matthew 21:21-22

We are living at the end of times, when great darkness is beginning to cover the face of the earth right before the return of Jesus Christ. If you allow this darkness to influence and penetrate your life, it could eventually lead you astray and completely destroy you. We are the generation that will see the physical return of the Lord back to earth. However, before this happens, we will see many horrible things take place in America and the world.

Many of the terrible things that are taking place on the earth today are not God's wrath, but the removal of His hedge of protection. Man's greed and his desire to play God using modern science, genetic manipulation and scalar technology are wreaking havoc on our ecosystem, and inflicting horrible devastation on our planet. God's wrath will come later during the great tribulation:

"And the nations were angry, and your wrath is come, and the time of the dead, that they should be judged, and that you should give reward unto your servants the prophets, and to the saints, and them that fear your name, small and great; and should destroy them who destroy the earth." Revelation 11:18

There is no doubt in my heart that we are in the very threshold of the fulfillment of all things that were spoken of by the prophets of old. Many great men of God would have liked to see this day, but God has given us the great privilege to be the ones to be alive today. The Lord has given me many dreams and visions concerning the Day of the Lord and the end of times. These dreams and visions are included in the last chapter of this book.

Chapter 7

STARTING A CHURCH

Sister Suzanne and her little boy had just moved from North Carolina to Miami, Florida to live with her parents. She had recently begun attending our church in North Miami at the same time we were about to leave to start the church in Miami. She had become good friends with us, so as soon as she found out we were leaving to start a church near to where she lived with her parents; she felt the Lord deal with her about coming along to help us.

Her parents owned an old house in the area of Little Havana that needed a lot of repairs. They agreed to rent it us for just $150 a month if we would do all the repairs and painting that it needed before we moved in. After we prayed about it, we accepted their offer. After all, we did not have many options on the table, and it was in a very good location. My parents lived only four blocks away, so they also could attend church if they liked.

However, the chance of my mother and brother, who were devout Catholics and my dad who was an agnostic ever setting foot on that little church, was remote. So we went to work on the house right away. The first thing we did was knock down a partition wall between the living room and dining room so we could have enough room to seat approximately twenty five people. We painted the walls, and put in a large window air conditioner.

We built a platform, where the pastor or any other person would be able to stand behind a huge pulpit that a church had donated. We bought twenty five chairs, a guitar, an amplifier, a microphone and a stand. I had a welder build me a baptismal tank to specifications so it would fit through the door, and we bought a pool ladder to get into the tank. We did not purchase a water heater because it was a bit too expensive for our budget.

We only had five present in our first service: Suzanne, her little boy Marcus, Yvette, a small stray dog and me. I played the guitar, we sang, we worshipped the Lord and we all had a great time in His presence. I am not going to tell you that those first few months were easy or that I was completely happy with the results; but I can tell you that the Lord always honored our faith and hard work with His presence, and His blessing remained with us.

By the end of that first year around Christmas time, I became so desperate to see someone saved and baptized that I gave a street bum some money if he would come to church with me. I managed to get a confession of faith out of him and quickly; before he had a chance to react, I persuaded him to be water baptized. We asked him to change into one of the white robes that we had bought, and up the ladder he went into my brand new water tank.

Everyone became extremely happy as we began to sing and clap our hands in anticipation of our very first water baptism. However, the celebration would have to wait. The moment his big toe touched the ice cold water, he let out a scream and started to climb back out of the tank. Right away, a wrestling match ensued between the bum trying to get out of the tank, and me trying to stop him from making his wish come true. It was a riot.

The more I tried to persuade him that it was all in his head, and that the water would get warmer once he got into the tank, the more desperate he became to get out of there. Suddenly he began to panic, probably thinking that we were some kind of cult or something. It slowly began to dawn on me that I was not going to be able to baptize him that night, so I let the bum go.

I had learned my lesson. I asked the Lord to forgive me for trying to force the poor bum to do something he was not quite ready for. If I would have had a water heater in the tank, maybe the story would have ended differently. We'll never know. After that, I just decided to do what I could do, and leave the results up to Him. We began to grow in size slowly, as people began to hear about the new church in the area and started to come.

After spending several weeks giving a bible study to Suzanna's parents, Roberto and Migdalia, in their home, they both began attending our church services and really seemed to enjoy it. After all, it was their own property, and their daughter and grandson were there as well. One day during service, the Holy Spirit got a hold of Migdalia and she was slain in the spirit. She became so drunk in the spirit that she could barely stand on her own feet.

She told me that she wanted to be baptized in water and receive the baptism of the Holy Spirit. We quickly prepared her for water baptism, and when I baptized her she received the Holy Spirit right there in the water tank; she began to speak in other tongues as the Spirit gave the utterance. I finally had my first water baptism, but this time it was by the power of the Holy Spirit:

"Then he answered and spoke unto me, saying, This is the word of the Lord unto Zerubbabel, saying, Not by might, nor by power, but by my spirit, says the Lord of hosts." Zechariah 4:6

"And they were all filled with the Holy Spirit, and began to speak with other tongues, as the Spirit gave them utterance." Acts 2:4

Her husband Roberto soon followed her into the waters of baptism; he also received the gift of the Holy Spirit and spoke in tongues as I baptized him. Suzanna became as happy as a termite in a yoyo, seeing her dreams come true right before her eyes, as both of her parents were saved and filled with the Holy Spirit. These events were important in that they served as a confirmation that God was with us, encouraging us to continue forward.

"Then Peter said unto them, Repent, and be baptized every one of you in the name of Jesus Christ for the remission of sins, and you shall receive the gift of the Holy Spirit. For the promise is unto you, and to your children, and to all that are afar off, even as many as the Lord our God shall call." Acts 2:38-39

A couple that I had won to the Lord (Rudy and Annie) had stopped attending the old church and grown cold. When I heard about it, I went to visit them in their home and after praying for them, told them we had started a church in Miami, and that I really needed their help. As they began attending services regularly, the Lord ignited the fire in them that had gone out. They both began to grow in the spirit, and Rudy became a blessing to me.

I discerned that he was ministry material, so I started to train and teach him the basic foundational principles of ministry, showing him by example, as well as providing him with books and resources that I believed would help him in his overall development. After a while, I began to give him plenty of opportunities to preach and use what he was learning, as he slowly began to improve steadily and blossom right before my eyes.

He started teaching people home bible studies along with me, and soon we began reaping the fruit from those efforts as people began to get converted and come to our church. During this time, my wife became pregnant with our first child Charis. We had been married now for three years, and our family was beginning to ask us when we were going to have a baby with increasing frequency. We prayed about it, and decided that it was the right time.

We both wanted our first child to be a girl, and prayed that she would be born with light colored eyes like both of her grandmothers. My mother had the most beautiful blue eyes, and my mother in law also has beautiful green eyes. Charis was born in May 14, 1986 with blue/green eyes and golden blonde hair, and right away she began to be spoiled by the members of the church.

We always took her with us everywhere we went; no baby sitters for us.

Revival Comes

Richard, a young man who worked at the Versailles Restaurant, heard about us and started attending our church. He had been converted in Nicaragua, along with his whole family, and had moved to Miami, Florida.   The Lord used him to bring many people to the church. He was instrumental in bringing his sister and brother in law, Marina and Reynaldo, who began attending all our church services and soon became a part of our group.

Richard also brought to church with him a Costa Rican waiter from the restaurant where he worked named Jose, as well as another young man from Uruguay who washed dishes named Gregory. He was baptized and received the Holy Spirit right away, while Jose rekindled the fires of his first love when he was born again in Costa Rica. They both became an integral part of the church. Later Marina brought her two brothers and two sisters who were lost.

There was this young man from Nicaragua named Juan who regularly came around in front of the church walking with his buddies, and would laugh at us whenever we tried to witness to him. We began to pray and intercede for him, and slowly the Lord began to deal with his heart. Because they were both from Nicaragua, Juan and Marina became friends, and eventually it became possible for her to give him a Bible study in her home.

One day he came to church and told me that that he was ready to be baptized and receive the Holy Spirit. We prayed with him, prepped him for water baptism and then proceeded to baptize him. As he came out of the water he was gloriously filled with the Holy Spirit and began to speak with other tongues. When he came out of the tank he was glowing with the Holy Spirit. I knew then that the Lord was going to use this boy in a great way.

In the following weeks, Juan single handedly brought a dozen people to the Lord, including his own family. He had an evident gift of leadership and evangelism. He had the rare ability to share the gospel with people in such a way, that he captured their interest immediately. He was then able to bring them to church where they were converted. He started going out into the street corners preaching the gospel with a bullhorn that we had bought.

We had been coming together for prayer for some time now on Friday nights from 7 pm until midnight. However, we all felt that we needed a breakthrough. So, we came together and planned a three day fast on a long holiday weekend coming up, and end it with an all night prayer meeting. We had all done one day fasts and partial fasts before, but none of us had ever done a three day fast.

The first night of prayer and fasting went well, without any problem. Everyone was real excited, and expectation was running high. On the second night I began to notice that the people were getting somewhat quieter, and their prayers were not as loud. The fast was beginning to take its toll on us all. By the time the third night came around, everyone started saying: "Tonight is the night when we break the fast, right Pastor?" I could not help but laugh.

By 3 am that night, some of the guys came ganging up on me, saying that they could not take it any more, if we could please end the fast. Jose, a funny Costa Rican, said to me: "Pastor, if I don't eat something soon, I am about to eat my mustache." I was so weak I could barely laugh at his joke. With a sigh, like a father letting his kids get away with it, I said "OK". They quickly left to buy steak sandwiches for everyone. What a way to break a fast.

Soon after, we began experiencing revival as people began getting saved, baptized and filled with the Holy Spirit in every service. Healings and miracles were taking place, and the presence and power of God was present every time we met. We began to grow so fast that later on that same year in 1986, God supplied us with a store front for about $300 a month, so we could accommodate all the people that were coming to our church services.

It was in a good location, only a few blocks away in the area of Little Havana, at the corner of Flagler Street and 17th Avenue. It had a seating capacity for about seventy people. We built a much bigger platform, bought better sound equipment and put in a large window a/c unit. Someone donated the carpeting for the whole place, and two of the guys who were gifted painters, drew two beautiful paintings on the walls containing scriptures.

We continued the revival there as the people continued to come to the church services and be saved. We stayed in that building for about a year, as we continued to grow in numbers and in stature. During that time, God brought to us additional pieces that would eventually become key components of our core group. Leonel, a young man from Nicaragua who had gotten cold in the Lord, came to one of the services and was re-filled with the Holy Spirit.

He quickly blended in with other young men we had from Nicaragua, so he felt at home right away. Sometime later, Rudy and Annie brought this family to church which they had been working with through a home bible study. There was the mother Lourdes, along with her daughter Martha, and her brother Alex. They all were baptized in water and received the Holy Spirit in the baptismal tank.

Alex became one of the most dependable workers in the church, and an intercessor. He did whatever I would ask him to do, and never missed a service. During this same time, Rudy was teaching a home bible study to one of his Cuban co-workers named Pete. I baptized him and he also was gloriously filled with the Holy Spirit right in the baptismal tank. Eventually, he became an important key leader in our church as the youth pastor.

We continued to grow and enjoy the presence of God in every way possible. I continued to work full time and pastor the church. The people were being blessed, and it seemed that everyone was genuinely enjoying coming to church and worshipping the Lord. We had prophecy, tongues and interpretation in almost every service as God continued to confirm our ministry with signs following. We had favor with God, and with the people.

A New Challenge

During that time Lewis Morley, who was pastoring a church in Hialeah, had become very ill and told me that he had decided to step down as pastor from that church. That came as a great shock to me. He had two young assistants in the church that had been helping him for some time, and I thought that he probably would leave one of them as the pastor. However, he didn't trust either of them, and they were also having personal problems.

When Morley told them both that they were not being considered as candidates to replace him as pastor of the church, they both packed up and left him. On top of that, the church was having some problems paying their high monthly rent of about $1,300 for the facilities that they were using. All of this had been taking a toll for some time on his fragile health. He was not a young person and his health was not getting better either.

One day he called me and told me that he needed to talk to me, so he asked me to come preach for him in the morning service, and afterwards took us out to lunch. At lunch he shared with me the situation he was facing, and told me that God had put on his heart that I was the one to take over his church. I told him that I already was pastoring a church, and that what he was asking was not possible. But he insisted, telling me to just sleep on it.

Because he was my mentor and spiritual father, I told him that I would sleep on it, and let him know one way or another in a few days. When I started to think about it, I began to feel in my heart sorry for him and for the sheep in that church. I began to realize that I could not say no to him. I was going to have to take over that church and pastor it, along with the one that I was already pastoring. So I called him up and told him that I would accept.

Immediately, I felt a burden come upon my shoulder that was not there before. The thought came to me that maybe I had made a big mistake, but I quickly dismissed that idea as being from the devil. After all, how could this not be from the Lord? That church had around thirty five members, about ten or so less than we had in our church. Between the two churches, we would have around eighty members. What was there not to like about that?

Besides, the Lord had been dealing with me for a while about leaving my secular job, and becoming a pastor full time. This seemed like an answer to my prayers from the Lord. However, some time later as I was in prayer, the Spirit of the Lord said to me: "Why are you doing what I did not ask you to do?" I could not understand why God would be telling me this; it just did not make any sense to me, until many years later.

After all, I was doing what he had called me to do. I was preaching the gospel saving the lost, and had started the church that he had asked me to. I had even left my full time job and was now only doing part time work. The more I racked my brain trying to make sense of what the Lord had said, the less sense it made. The only person I knew who could have possibly provided me with godly counsel was the very one who had asked for my help.

I was about to learn a very important lesson in my ongoing training; the consequences of missing God, and going through open doors that He never meant for me to go through. I did not understand that sometimes in life, there are some things which may appear good to the natural man, even noble. However, if it is not the will of God, it will cause much suffering, pain and untold misery. This is something most people only learn by experience.

"For my thoughts are not your thoughts, neither are your ways my ways, says the Lord. For as the heavens are higher than the earth, so are my ways higher than your ways, and my thoughts than your thoughts." Isaiah 55:8-9

Most Christians do not understand that the yoke the Lord has for us is easy, because it is personally designed and tailored made for each one of us. If you come under a yoke that the Lord never intended for you to carry, it will hurt you and weigh you down because you were not meant to do that or carry that load. The Lord will not help you carry a load if you do what He did not ask you to do.

"Come unto me, all you that labor and are heavy laden, and I will give you rest. Take my yoke upon you, and learn of me; for I am meek and lowly in heart: and you shall find rest unto your souls. For my yoke is easy, and my burden is light." Matthew 11:28-30

When the time came for us to take over as pastors of the church in Hialeah, we brought the Miami church over that Sunday morning and held a combined service. There was much rejoicing and celebration that morning among the people. However, I noticed that there were several of his people that apparently didn't seem to approve of me. Since Morley was the founder of that church, he did not have to submit his choice to a vote by the congregation.

The only problem with that was that now I was stuck with a situation in that church that I neither asked for nor wanted. However, it was too late for me to back out, so I resigned myself to do the best I could with it and leave the rest to God. After praying about how to pastor both churches simultaneously, I decided the only way to do it was to have both churches together on Sunday morning in Hialeah, then have the evening service in Miami.

Since most members of the church in Hialeah were old people, they did not come out to be with us on Sunday evening services in Miami. Only a handful ever came out to be with us and support us. Everything else seemed to be working alright for the moment. Morley had been able to secure some financial help from home missions to help with the rent for a while, but that help would run out in a few months. After that, we were on our own.

As time went on, I began to face increasing criticisms from the Hialeah Church people. Some of them began to say that I did not have enough experience to pastor that church, while others believed that I had not been saved long enough to pastor them. Apparently, they didn't seem to care or consider the fact that I had raised a church up from nothing, while working a full time job at that. Little did I realize that I was fighting a demonic religious spirit.

This spirit did not manifest completely, nor do its deadly work until later on, after it had enough time to contaminate a big part of the congregation. This religious spirit wanted to preserve, at any cost, its way of life, mindset, paradigms and traditions. It felt threatened by us because we were a bit different from them and they began to attack us viciously and without mercy. Most of them did not lift a finger to help us, but instead wasted their time finding fault with us.

A religious spirit inflates people with pride. The leaven in bread does not add substance or any nutritional value to the bread; its only real purpose is to inflate it. Likewise, the religious spirit does not add any good thing to the church; it only feeds self-sufficiency and pride. The Lord will not inhabit or use anything that Satan has inflated through pride, and the devil knows that once leaven gets into bread, it is very difficult to remove (2Timothy 3:5; Romans 10:2-11).

Along with pride, the religious spirit is the most difficult stronghold to correct or remove because of its very nature. Believers will never be able to worship God in spirit and in truth until they are free from this deception. This spirit deludes people into believing that God is just like them, thus blocking out rebukes, exhortations, or correction, believing that they are for other people, and not for them.

Real humility can only come as a result of a true revelation of God's mercy and grace, which is the only true antidote for the religious spirit. Whenever the Lord compares the religious spirit to the leaven of the Pharisees, it is because they are very similar in how they operate and what they do (Matthew 16:12; Luke 12:1-2). The Pharisees and Sadducees were worshiping traditions more than God.

When the Lord did not come having the same regard for their traditions, they persecuted Him. That is the reason why the Pharisees, who loved the Word of God along with their traditions and were hoping for the coming of the Messiah more than anyone else, rejected and persecuted Jesus when He visited them in Israel. They were not about to let Him do a work among them. So, like it happened back then, it was happening again. Only, I was the victim this time.

Chapter 8

THE PASTORATE

As we continued to pastor both churches and travel back and forth every Sunday and Wednesday night, it became clear to me that it was beginning to take a toll on me and my wife, the church and the finances. There was no way that we could keep this for much longer. I talked with my boss about my situation and asked him if there was any way that I could cut back my total work hours a week from forty to thirty. He thought about it for a moment, and quickly said yes.

We had a meeting with the leaders of the church and reached a unanimous decision that it would be in the best interests of everyone to consolidate both churches, and use only one building. Since the church facility in Hialeah was bigger than the one in Miami, and it had a large parking space available, we decided that we would use that one, dispensing with the building in Miami.

Everyone accepted that decision, although I could tell by the looks on some of their faces that they were sad to see the Miami facility shut down, but I had no choice. I did not have a minister ready yet to be able to take over it, and I did not relish the idea of pastoring the Hialeah church by itself. Besides that, the financial help coming from Home Missions had ended, and now in order to pay the rent of $1,300 for the facilities in Hialeah, something was going to have to give.

In addition, because my salary had been cut whenever I asked for a reduction in my weekly hours, I was beginning to have problems meeting my monthly family expenses. There was a one bedroom apartment right next to the church facility that was occupied by a couple that was a member of the Hialeah church. When they were told that they would have to move so that we could occupy it, they did not like that too much; like we needed more wood added to the fire.

The apartment was much smaller than the two bedroom house we were renting before, and not as pretty; but we would be able to save the money on the rent and utilities. I continued to work a secular job while the church grew, as I was not drawing a salary as a pastor. We replaced an orange carpet that was there with a brand new blue commercial carpet; painted the walls of the church, and installed new a/c ducts and vents throughout the ceiling the auditorium.

Some of the young men put fresh popcorn on the ceiling. Others sanded and painted the old pulpit that was there, and when they brought it back, it looked brand new. Our gifted painter painted a beautiful mural of a waterfall behind the platform which was beautiful. We also built a beautiful sign in front of the church eight feet high, made of blocks and cement. We covered it with dark blue tiles, and then put the church name and phone number in white plastic letters.

We also ran electric wires to the sign and put a couple of spot lights so it would be lit up at nights. We did whatever we could to make the church facilities look nice, and the people comfortable. I studied for hours during the week, and prepared for each service like I was going to the largest church in the city. I never did hold back from them. I visited all the ones that were backslidden, and gave them a home bible study. Many of their children began to come to church.

Our Miami people loved my preaching and teaching, but the Hialeah members were not used to it. They were used to short messages and services. Their wineskins were smaller and drier. My wife told me that I was feeding them too much meat; actually, I thought that I was not giving them enough. I would always minister to the people after the message, and prayed for them according to their needs. There were always some that were saved, healed and filled with the Holy Spirit.

They had put their baptismal tank right in the auditorium, so whenever the people were baptized in water, they had togo to the bathroom which was in the apartment that we were living in now. They had these plastic runners that they placed on the carpet whenever people were baptized so it would not get wet. One day we were going to baptize a young man who was married to one of the girls in the church. I taught him a home bible study, and now he was ready to be baptized.

The young man who always helped us with the baptisms was not there that morning, so I asked someone else to get everything ready. After I performed the baptism, everyone was rejoicing when he came out of the tank. Then, as he began walking on the plastic runner heading back to the bathroom, all of a sudden, he began skipping and hollering: "Ooh, ah"! The people thought that it was a blessing from God, and everyone began to praise the Lord even louder.

However, that wasn't really what was going on at all. You see, the plastic runners were really nice and smooth on the side that the people were supposed to walk on, but on the reverse side they had these sharp spikes that were supposed to keep the plastic runner from slipping on top of the carpet. The young man that always did the baptisms knew that, but the new guy did not. When we realized what was going on, we all started laughing, that is except the man walking on it.

Going on the Radio

As the finances slowly began to increase, we were able to meet all our expenses and still have some money left over. One day, a door of opportunity opened up for us to have a radio program in a local radio station. It was only fifteen minutes every day and very expensive, but I felt that it was the right time for us to throw the net out there. At first, the response from the people was not great, and some church people started saying that it was a waste of money.

However, being the stubborn man that I am, I refused to give in to their criticisms and quit. As we continued sowing the seed into the city with the radio program, we slowly began to see the results that we had anticipated when we started. We also began taking phone calls during and after the radio shows, which allowed us to make connection with a lot of people. We began building a large listening audience within the Christian community in the city.

Christians from other congregations began attending our services, as they were looking for the presence and power of the Holy Spirit, and were also being fed by the teachings we were sharing. They were coming mostly from the traditional churches that didn't practice the gifts of the Holy Spirit in their services. Whenever they came to visit us, we quickly offered them a home bible study and followed through by visiting them and teaching them in their homes once a week.

By now we had several trained young people able to teach home bible studies, but Pete and I did most of them. We would each do two or three home bible studies a week. On the weekends, he would rent a van with his own money and pick up all the people on his home bible studies and bring them to church. Many times he brought a van full of people with him to church. Most of them were saved, baptized and filled with the Holy Spirit, and we seldom lost any of them.

The Home Bible Studies served not only as a means to get people saved, but also as a great discipleship tool. Being able to go to the home of a family for twelve consecutive weeks helped us to get to know them really well, and to build strong relationships and trust. I am really convinced that this was what made the radio ministry so successful. Having the radio show by itself, was not enough to get the people to make a commitment to serve the Lord in the local church.

The following year, a door opened in another radio station for us to have more time. This radio station was much more powerful than the previous one, and would allow us to reach all of Dade County and part of Broward. They gave us a great deal for thirty minutes a day, five days a week at noon. This was an opportunity too good to pass. It was more expensive but now that I had the experience, I was confident that we would be able to pay for the expenses one way or another.

I went around to some of the local businesses to secure some sponsors for the program. We managed to get a couple of sponsors that would help pay for the additional cost of the radio programs. Several of our members also had pledged to support the radio programs with weekly contributions. As we continued to do the programs, the harvest of souls continued to come in. Later that same year, we were offered a whole hour for the same money at 12 midnight which we took.

My wife and little two year old girl would go with me every night to the radio station and we would bring a little mattress so Charis could sleep there. My wife would take the phone calls in another room, while I conducted the program. Yvette became real good at it, learning how to filter out the nasty crank calls so we could concentrate on the ones coming from good people needing prayer. She wrote their information down on a piece of paper, and we would call them later.

By the time we finished taking all the phone calls and got back to our home, it was around 2 am in the morning. This was taking a toll on us, but it was worth it all. We saw a lot of people saved during that time and many miracles take place. One night a young homosexual man who was dying of AIDS, called us telling us that he was going to commit suicide. We prayed for him and asked him to visit our church.

We were surprised to see him come during that midweek service, as he gave his life to God, was baptized and received the Holy

Spirit. Then we gathered around him and cast that spirit of AIDS out of him. God delivered him that night. He was not the only ex-homosexual person that we had in the church. We had three guys and three gals who were serving the Lord with us who had been delivered from that lifestyle.

Revival was breaking out as our church attendance was now running around 120 people on Sunday morning. During that time, I felt that enough finances was coming in that I could quit working my secular job and dedicate all my time to the work of the ministry. When I talked to my boss, he did not want me to quit at all. Even years later, he would call me and ask me to come back to work for him again.

Even though I loved working for him and the money was really great, I knew in my heart that the Lord wanted me to work full time for him. The pay was not as good, but the benefits were beyond this world. Besides, I was having such a good time enjoying the revival that I did not miss the extra cash. My wife deserves some credit, as she never complained about the downsizing of our lifestyle throughout this process.

One day while revival was taking place, the Lord brought me face to face with my first deliverance case. Although I had read and heard about deliverance, I had absolutely no experience in this field. She was a beautiful young girl who had been totally demonized. Her face was all contorted and disfigured; both her eyes were tearing, and her left arm kept shaking as if she was suffering from Parkinson's disease.

The parents told me that days before, she had attempted to witness to a Brujo in his Botanica in the city of Miami. She was ignorant of the powers of darkness, and had never been taught about these things. She thought that it would be safe to do this, when in reality she was entering into a lion's den. After she witnessed to him the Brujo disappeared into a back room and returned later with a cigar in his mouth, blowing smoke in her face and speaking some gibberish out loud.

After she had left his place, she began feeling somewhat confused, as if something weird was happening to her. By the time she got home, a demon of insanity had taken over her mind as she went into a fit of rage and started to throw things around. An ambulance had to come and place her in a restraining jacket to take her to the hospital. When the doctor saw her, he told the parents that she had totally lost her mind, and would never recover her sanity again.

The doctor then prescribed her some sedatives to keep her calm, and told her parents to take her home and just keep her sedated. They took her to many churches and faith healers in hopes that somehow she would be healed and set free, but they were not successful. As she kept getting worse and worse, one day her parents heard me on the radio and decided to bring her to us. The minute that I saw her walk through the door, I could sense the demonic oppression.

When I began ministering to her, I could tell that what she really needed was deliverance, not healing. So, I asked her father and mother to bring her back the next day so we could minister deliverance to her. The next day we spent about two hours ministering to her without any results; so I stopped and asked the Holy Spirit to reveal to me what was hindering her from being set free. The other intercessors kept praying in the room, while I was receiving instruction from the Lord.

When the Holy Spirit showed me what the problem was, I confronted her with it and she immediately repented. Then I prayed over her for the healing of her emotions. As healing began taking place with tears flowing, I then confronted the evil spirit and commanded it to leave in the name of Jesus as she began retching and vomited this yellowish substance that had a horrible smell. When this process had been completed, I then asked her to worship the Lord and thank Him.

As she began to worship God her face returned to normal, her eyes stopped tearing and the shaking in her arm ceased. It was a miracle; however the father did not seem convinced as he reached into his pocket and took out a bottle of pills the doctor had prescribed her. When I saw it, I told him to put it away because she was healed. The next day as they all came to service he came through the door first and said in loud voice: "Praise the Lord, my daughter is healed."

That night there was great victory in God's house as their daughter came forth and shared her complete testimony. Her face was radiant and full of the glory of the Lord as she sang praises unto God. Everyone present rejoiced and glorified theGod of heaven for his great and miraculous deliverance. After she shared her testimony in church, she also shared it on the radio. This was heard by a lot of people that were suffering from demonic oppression, and they also began to come.

As the anointing of God began to increase in our ministry, these demonic spirits would sometimes manifest right in the services. One time this woman came with her daughter to church. When the presence of God began to manifest, so did the demonic spirit within her. She began to roll her head like a windmill, and let out a scream that sent chills down my spine, as her hair which was contained in a bun, flew out.

As she kept doing this, some of the people that were present in service thought that she was getting blessed by the Lord, but I knew better. I told her that I needed to talk to her after service. When I began to question her about her past, she told me that she had come out of witchcraft. She had been truly converted, baptized and filled with Holy Spirit, yet she was still severely demonized.

This was the second case in one month where I had seen a spirit filled Christian who was demonized. The Lord was bringing me into a ministry of deliverance and was beginning to shed some light and revelation in this area. One day as mall middle-aged Cuban man brought his mother to our church. During the service, the power of God came upon him and he was thrown down, shaking and convulsing.

We took him to a little room in the back of the church, which we had nicknamed "the clinic." While we were ministering to him, we found out that he used to be a very famous spiritist in Cuba. People would wait outside his home to be first in line to see him the next day. He used to be called "the prodigy child of Guanabo," due to his clairvoyant abilities.

He was able to tell the people what was going on in their lives, and foretell their future. The same day we cast four spirits out of him that regularly manifested through him. He has been free ever since and serving the Lord. The news spread like wildfire, and pretty soon we had to begin training others in the ministry of deliverance because of the number of people that continually came seeking help.

This caused other pastors in the area to become fearful and jealous, as they began to attack us on the radio. They were afraid that some of their sheep would leave and come to our church, so they began trying to use smear tactics to scare people, calling us a false cult, and many other things. I never used the radio to retaliate in kind, and never tried to steal their sheep. I just did my job; my heart was at peace.

A Revelation of His Grace

It was during this time that I crossed paths with a pastor who had a radio show right before us. His ministry was one that stressed the grace of God. He was easily one of the best teachers I have ever met on the subject of grace. This was something that we desperately needed in our lives, as the denomination that we were associated with was extremely legalistic and dogmatic, bordering on a cult.

They believed that anyone who did not believe and live like they did was not saved. This caused us a lot of problems with other churches, and eventually many good people left and went to other churches. If many of the people that left us and went to other churches because of these issues would have stayed, they would probably number in the hundreds. However, this was all part of God's master plan for my life.

One day my wife and I went to a conference in the state of Maryland hosting some of the best preachers and teachers on the cutting edge in the area of the supernatural and other areas of divine revelation. I enjoyed every one of the topics and the speakers, but there was one in particular that really impacted me; his name was C. R. Free. He talked about the grace of Jesus Christ and how the revelation of His grace had changed his life forever. This was the scripture that he used:

"And of his fullness have we all received, and grace for grace. For the law was given by Moses, but grace and truth came by Jesus Christ." John 1:16-17

After he finished sharing his message, he closed by saying this: "My name is Free, but I was not free." Then to top it all off, the pastor of the church hosting the conference Chester Wright, took the microphone from him and said: "And my name is Wright, but I was wrong." You could hear a pin drop after these two men were done. Needless to say, that this message had left a lasting impression upon me and most of the people there. However, the best was yet to come

When I got back to the hotel after lunch, we laid down for a nap before the evening service. As I was resting, I had an experience I had never had before. The Lord spoke to me in a powerful voice that resounded throughout my whole being, and said to me: "Why are you trying to do in the flesh, what I already did at the cross of Calvary?" He said this to me three times, and then I woke up. As I woke up, I could still hear His words resounding through my whole being.

This experience, along with what this man had shared, stayed with me for a very long time even after we got back home. It impacted my life to such an extent that blindfolds that had been a part of me for years began to fall. As I began to study scriptures and learn more and more about grace, paradigms and mindsets in me began to fall as the Lord began to reveal His wonderful grace to me. It felt like I had been born again, all over again.

Whole books that I had never really fully understood like the book of Romans, Corinthians, Galatians, Ephesians, Hebrews, Philippians, Colossians and others, now all of a sudden began to make sense to me. I would spend hours a day, studying the scriptures that talked about His grace. I subscribed to John MacArthur's Bible School Library and listened to all of his teachings on cassette dealing with all the New Testament books, especially the ones mentioned above.

The more I learned about grace, the more I realized how wrong we were in many of the teachings that we had been teaching the people in church. I had always felt in the past that there was something missing. The denomination had some teachings in the area of holiness that, although I faithfully taught them in church, I didn't feel too comfortable teaching them and knew that there was something wrong.

One of the holiness standards was that women could not cut their hair, paint their nails, and wear any makeup or jewelry like earrings, rings, necklaces or any other thing. Needless to say, the women were quite miserable in complying with all these man made commandments. In addition, they were not able to wear any pants; no, not even in winter. Forget about bathing suits or any decent shorts. They would go straight to hell if they did. I had been putting a burden on God's people that they could not carry.

I would even keep tabs if anyone saw any of the sisters out in the street that had violated any of these so called standards of holiness, and made sure to take away their privileges when they came to church. I was a modern day Pharisee, and did not know it. Ignorance is bliss, and I was definitely enjoying my ignorance during all those years. But the worst part is that I thought I was pleasing the Lord, without realizing that He was disgusted with it.

A Split in The Church

Slowly I began teaching grace to the church, but I noticed right away that it was not going to go over very well. Some seemed to receive it right away, but most struggled with it and were never able to receive the revelation and make the transition, especially those that were not a part of our Miami church. They began to criticize me for the things that I was teaching the church concerning grace, and say unkind things about me and my wife. This kept going on for a while.

After a while, I noticed that a click began forming among those who were against me teaching grace, as they always sat together and you could feel a strong resistance coming from them. Some of them were in a position of leadership in the church including Rudy, my own spiritual son. He had been contaminated by the leaven of the Pharisees, as the devil began to work on him overtime. I noticed that he began coming late to service, and sometimes did not make it at all.

When I asked him about it, he just shrugged his shoulders and said that he was very busy. Others, who were confused and undecided on the issue of grace, decided that they were going to side with him and began getting an attitude towards me. I did not know however, how serious this situation was until much later. I found out that they were secretly meeting in one of their homes once a week, and scheming what they were going to do. This was just too much for me to take.

I arranged a meeting with Rudy in private and shared with him my concerns. He answered me bluntly, and in cold terms told me about his plans to leave the church in the very near future because I was not preaching and practicing holiness anymore. When he told me that, I was so shocked I could barely stand. I had never experienced anything like this, and was not ready for what came out of his mouth. Rudy was the last one I would ever have expected to betray me this way.

I had brought him and his whole family to the Lord, and personally laid hands on him to receive the Holy Spirit; I taught him everything he knew, even helping him to become a preacher. I loved him like my own son. I thought he would at least allow me the opportunity to explain some things and be willing to exercise some patience throughout the whole process while we worked things out. I thought he owed me that much. However, he had already made up his mind.

When the day of his departure finally arrived, I let him go and wished him the best, thinking that this would be the end of the matter. A short time after he left however, members of the click began to come in one by one to inform me of their decision to go and join him start another church. Every one of them took their turn in coming to me and telling me. I knew that evil spirits were behind it, and there was nothing that I could do to stop it. This was a trial I had to endure.

By the time they were done, we had lost one third of the church members, along with the assistant pastor, the youth pastor, and several other leaders in the church. The church never fully recovered from this death blow. We continued to preach to gospel, people continued to be saved, healed and delivered; we continued to hold many revivals and saw many miracles at the hand of the Lord, but it was never the same.

My wife suffered a nervous breakdown that has affected her even to this day. I burned out and went through severe bouts of depression, to the point where I almost quit the ministry altogether. Evil spirits in the form of owls began to torment me and mock me, as I began to see owls coming to me, no matter where I was, and just sit there looking at me. It was the most bizarre thing I have ever experienced. I was facing another test; this one had to do with forgiveness:

"Should you not also have had compassion on your fellow servant, even as I had pity on you? And his lord was wroth, and delivered him to the tormentors, till he should pay all that was due unto him. So likewise shall my heavenly Father do also unto you, if you from your hearts forgive not every one his brother their trespasses." Matthew 18:33-35

I am not going to lie and tell you that it was easy forgiving Rudy. It took every bit of will and determination coupled with the grace of God to forgive him. However, after months of dealing with this issue, I was finally able to pray for him and ask the Lord to bless him without feeling any hatred, anger or bitterness towards him. I released him and all the people that left with him to the lord, and went on with my life.

I began to travel conducting revivals all through the land, as we continued to pastor the church. Slowly I began to see a difference in my ministry when I traveled, and noticed that it was not the same when I was pastoring in the local church. I began going into long periods of fasting and prayer seeking the Lord for answers. One day I was conducting a revival in an Assembly of God church in Miami Beach. God moved with signs following as there was an outpouring of the Holy Spirit.

There was a man of God there from Brazil who had done a revival for them the week before whose name was Rodolfo Beautenmueller. He had a worldwide ministry of signs and wonders. I invited him to come and preach in our church the following week, and we had a tremendous service. I forgot all about it until several weeks later. I kept seeking the Lord in fasting and prayer for a word. I did a few fasts 21 days long, a couple 30 days fast and I even did a 40 day fast once.

One day as I was praying, the Lord spoke to me and told me to go speak to Rodolfo Beautenmueller, that he would give me word. As I called him up and went to visit him, the first thing he said to me was: "You are out of place." He told me that when he saw me ministering in Miami Beach, and then came to preach for me and saw me pastoring there, he knew that I was not supposed to be pastoring there. He said that God had a worldwide ministry for me similar to his.

He then told me that if I did not obey the Lord, eventually I would have to put a padlock on the door of the church as it would be shut down. I had a feeling He would say something like that however, now there was no doubt. I began to make preparations to obey God right away. The attendance of the church began to go down, and I dreaded whenever I had to be home pastoring the church. I started to go on revival trips often, and they became longer and longer each time.

The more I went on the road, the more the people began to skip church and hold back on their tithes and offerings. I realized that this could not go on for much longer. My heart was no longer in pastoring the church there, and I knew that the people needed a full time pastor. I had trouble sleeping at night, and would wake up real early in the morning with a burden in my heart. I felt as if the Lord had passed me over and left me behind. It was a horrible feeling of despair.

I decided to have a heart to heart talk with Papa, and tell him that I was ready to obey Him, no matter what. One day the Lord spoke to me and told me that he wanted me to learn to hear His voice clearly. He said that He was going to begin to talk to me more often, and that I needed to be able to hear His voice clearly so I could obey Him. Little did I realize what He was about to ask me to do.

Chapter 9

THE DAY OF RECKONING

My wife had opened a daycare to help with the finances, and for a couple of years she had now been operating it with fairly good success. She only had about 8-10 children, and most of them came from Christian parents. Some of them began attending our church, and eventually became some of the best members. We needed to use the apartment where we were living for the daycare, so we moved into one of the two bedroom duplexes at the front of the church property.

It was bigger than where we were living before, but the kitchen was much smaller. I bought some used furniture for the living room, put up new blinds on the windows, and my wife fixed up the place real nice as we settled in and lived there for over a year. We continued to run the church and daycare with diligence and excellence as we waited upon the Lord. Several weeks went by, and then one day it happened.

It was during the month of January in the winter of 1992, when my family and I had returned from a service. We had recently cancelled our Sunday evening services at church due to low attendance, and had started visiting other churches in the area in hopes of getting a word from the Lord. I retired to bed early that night, as I said my prayers and fell into a restful sleep. In the middle of the night I had a vision.

I saw a man preparing a picnic for me in the middle of the most beautiful prairie. The grass was dark green, the flowers were incredibly beautiful and the sky was a dark blue. The wind was blowing softly on my face and the sun was shining brightly in the sky. As I got closer to where the man was, He looked at me and suddenly began to speak to me in a voice that I had heard so many times before. It was the Lord.

As He kept talking to me I woke up still hearing His words. His presence was so strong in my room that I began to cry. He was telling me that it was time for me to leave. He asked me to resign as pastor, and turn the church over to another man. He told me to take my wife, my little girl and all our stuff and go to a place that He was going to show me. I tried to bargain with Him, asking Him if we could move to a city in Broward County just north of us.

He answered me however, and told me that it was not possible. He said that I needed to just keep going north to a place that He would show me. I said: "Where Lord, where do you want me to go?" He then reminded me that when He called Abraham out of Ur of Chaldea, he left not knowing where he was going, and he was blessed in a great way. He said that I also would be blessed, and that He would take care of me through His servants who hear His voice.

He said that I had been called to an end time ministry to prepare His Bride for His soon return, and that I was not the only one, but only one of many. I wrote everything He was saying down on a piece of paper as fast as I could. It was the middle of the night, but I had learned to write in the dark and had done it before, so it was not too hard. The Lord also said many other things to me which are personal, and I still hold very close to my heart to this day.

I do not know how long I spent on my knees talking to the Lord that night; all I know is that when the sun finally came up, I was in tears still talking to Him. Slowly as His presence began to lift, I was left alone in my room, with pages full of instruction. I quickly told my wife about the experience, and as I did I began to cry. The presence of God was filling the room once again. My wife didn't know what to say. However, she knew that I had been with the Lord that night.

It was not going to be easy to obey the Lord on this one. I had lived in Miami for over twenty six years, and had spent all of my youth there; both of my parents, my relatives and all my friends lived there; I had gone to school and worked there; had been saved and married there; we were running a church and daycare there, and now we were going to leave it all behind, and go to a place that God was going to show us.

When I went to tell my parents about my decision to resign as pastor of the church and leave Miami, they became very sad, especially my mother. She had become very ill and believed that she would probably never get to see me again. My father, who did not show his emotions often, was visibly shaken as he said to me with his voice breaking: "Do not forget about us". I just hugged them tight and kissed them as I tried to hold back my tears.

"Then Peter said: Lo, we have left all, and followed you. And he said unto them, Verily I say unto you, There is no man that has left house, or parents, or brethren, or wife, or children, for the kingdom of God's sake, Who shall not receive many times more in this present time, and in the world to come life everlasting." Luke 18:28-30

I knew that I had to obey the Lord no matter what. I tried to encourage them by telling them I would come to Miami to visit them often and that I might even take them to live with us eventually. However, deep in my heart I knew that would never happen, since they were both old and unlikely to move away from their family and friends. As people get older, it becomes increasingly more difficult for them to make drastic changes in life than when they are younger.

I began to move quickly in obedience to the instructions from the Lord and went to see the man that was supposed to take over as pastor of the church. He could not believe what he was hearing. He was very happy because he only had a handful of people in his church, and didn't even have a building where to meet. I held a special meeting in church where I informed the congregation about my plans to resign.

I could tell that most of them were genuinely sad to hear about the news, although a few were probably relieved to hear it. I introduced the new pastor to the congregation, and shortly after began having services together. The Lord began to send some of his prophets to us giving us many words of encouragement and confirmation regarding the things that He had spoken to me. It strengthened our faith to hear it.

The man I had left as pastor of the church tried to create problems for me to be sure that I would never be able to return and take the church back, even after I had repeatedly told him that I would never do that. The Lord had instructed me to sever all connections and ties with the church, as He made abundantly clear to me that I was not to retain any position in the church, although according to the church by- laws, as a founder of the church I had the right to do so.

This did not make the situation easier for me, as he began spreading rumors and lies about me among the people in the church, even turning some of them against me. The situation became so tense, that eventually we were not able to be in service with them. I started to preach in churches in the area just so I would not have to be there. I felt like David when he was hiding in caves, as he was being persecuted by his own son and those who were once his followers.

I committed my share of mistakes; most of them due to my lack of experience, and some due to my stupidity. They were all part of the learning process I had to endure, in order to be able to fulfill the ministry that the Lord had called me to do. When I was going through the pain and suffering of these trials, it was difficult for me to see how any good could come out of it. Only now do I see it, as I reflect upon it.

"Now no chastening for the present seems to be joyous, but grievous: nevertheless afterward it yields the peaceable fruit of righteousness unto them who are trained by it. Therefore lift up the hands which hang down, and the feeble knees." Hebrews 12:11-12

We decided to shut down the daycare and move back into the small apartment where we were before. We placed all our furniture into a storage warehouse, leaving only the beds we were sleeping in, along with my desk and file cabinet. We stayed there until the time when we would be ready to move out. The Lord had told me to go to the Prophetic Conference that was being held in Atlanta, where He would give me a word of confirmation through the prophets there.

The Adventure Begins

We left knowing we were going to Atlanta first, but had no idea where we would go next. I took my wife, my daughter, put all our luggage in my 1991 Honda Civic and took off. As soon as we arrived at the hotel, we dropped the luggage and went directly to the conference. When we arrived there, the place was completely filled with ministers and their families, and the atmosphere was charged with the presence of God as the choir was singing and worshipping the Lord.

There were two prophets that were ministering that night in the Conference. One was from New Jersey, and the other was from North Carolina. The latter has become a household name in the ranks of Christianity today; his name was Mark Chirona. When the altar call was made, they asked all of the ministers who wanted to receive a word from the Lord to come forward and stand around the altar.

As we made our way to the altar, there was a spot right in front of the pulpit which for some reason, no one had taken yet. It was as if the Lord kept that space for me until I got there. As my wife and

I stood there, they made a beeline to me as the Bishop from New Jersey came and laid his hands on my shoulder. The words that came out of his mouth were straight from the throne room of God. It was as if he knew the conversation that the Lord had with me.

Then after he finished, Mark Chirona picked up where he left off, and continued to confirm one thing after another. He then began to prophesy about future events that would take place in my life and ministry that I treasure even to this day. Everything that they both said has come to pass, as the Lord was faithful to His word. I had never experienced prophetic presbytery, and was totally awed by the experience.

This prophetic event served not only to confirm the word that the Lord had given me, but also as a catalyst to activate the gifts that were dormant inside of me. Therein lies the power of the prophetic word. It is able to do things that the preaching of the word, prayer or even fasting are not able to. I left there with a precious deposit in my spirit that would allow me to go to that next level in God that I had been so desperately seeking after for a long time.

After the Conference the pastor who was hosting it, Henry Jones, took us out to lunch where we had a chance to talk and have some fellowship. I shared with him what was going on in our lives, and that we were just trying to find the place that the Lord wanted us in. He asked us right away to move to Atlanta, and join his church. He said that I could use his church as a platform to launch my ministry nationwide.

He had a lot of connections, and his church was located in a large city which is considered the gateway to the south. We were offered other things as well, and told him that we would pray about it and let him know about our decision. However, although we liked some of the benefits of moving to the city of Atlanta and joining his church, the more we prayed about it, the more we became convinced that was not the place.

From the conference we went to visit a friend of mine who lived in the Smokey Mountains of Tennessee. Steve Grimsley had been in our church and preached several revivals for us. I really liked him, and we got along fairly well. We stayed a few days with him and his family, and he took me to one of the local churches on a Wednesday night where I preached. When I shared with him our situation, he quickly asked us to move up there and help him pastor a church.

He said that we could pastor a church together, and that we could take turns traveling conducting revivals nationwide, while the other one stayed behind and pastored the church. Although his idea had some merit, I did not feel comfortable going into pastoring again after what we had gone through, especially one that involved working with another ministry. I prayed about it, but I did not feel the peace of the Lord.

We said our good byes and went on to Christ Church in Nashville, Tennessee to be with our friend L.H. Hardwick. He was extremely kind and gracious to us. He got us a room in a local hotel, and asked me to share in their midweek service. As we talked to him several times and discussed our situation with him, he also asked us to move up there and be a part of his staff. He said that I could use his church as a home base for my ministry, and that his church would stand behind me.

This offer was extremely tempting, as Christ Church is one of the largest well known churches in the nation, running approximately 7,000 members or more on Sunday morning. I thanked him for his offer, and told him that I would seriously consider it. When I took it to prayer, God did not give me the green light. The more I prayed about it, the more I knew that was not the place where He wanted me.

On the way back home, we stopped in Columbus, Georgia to

preach for another nice church there. I ministered in both services as the Lord confirmed the word with signs following. Unknown to me was the fact that during the week, Hardwick had discussed our situation with the Pastor, and told him that maybe I was the man that he was looking for. After the morning service, the pastor took us out to lunch.

The church was located in an area of the city where there was a growing Spanish population. Many of them had started to come to his church, and he was looking for someone who would pastor the people. He shared that with me during lunch, and offered me the position. He was even willing to pay for all of our relocation and moving expenses. Again, I did not feel comfortable going into a situation where I would have to pastor a church, after what we had been through.

Besides, that church was still in the throes of legalism that we were just beginning to come out of, plus I would have to be under the authority of another pastor. That made it three strikes, so I did not even have to pray about this one. I was thankful that he had considered me, but we politely declined and went on our way. On our way to Atlanta, we had passed this city in North Central Florida called Live Oak. As we were going through it, I had felt a slight tug in my spirit.

As I had turned to my wife and asked her if she felt the same thing, she answered in the affirmative. We decided that on our way back, we were going to stop there again to check it out. So as we were coming back, we stopped in Live Oak and rented a hotel there for a whole week. We traveled over the whole area, checking the neighboring cities of Jasper, Madison, Branford, White Springs and Mayo.

However, the more we looked at the city of Live Oak, the more we liked it. We traveled it by car and on foot, stopping at certain areas and asking questions. The presence of the Lord grew stronger the more that we looked around. Finally, after much prayer, we decided to look for a place to live. As we continued to look, we saw this old but pretty white house right in the center of town.

It was a three bedroom, two bath house with a huge den and living room. It had a large walk-in closet in the master bedroom, and a carport for one vehicle. It also had a fireplace and a large room with a washer and drier. The owner was an old lady who lived alone. She wanted to move north to live with her son. She was asking for $34,000 which was a good price, especially when compared to Miami prices.

We had tried to buy a much larger piece of property for our church, since we had outgrown the place where we were. We had found a one acre plot in a nice area of Hialeah, but when we asked for the price, we were shocked at what they were asking for; the price tag was one million dollars. That, plus the fact that no bank wanted to loan us money, made it prohibitive; so we finally gave up owning our own property.

Anyway, that was water under the bridge as now we were about to buy our very own house for pennies to the dollar of what it would cost in Miami. We had never been able to buy our own home there because the prices were so expensive. This same house would have cost us way over $150,000 in Miami, Florida. I had enough for the $5,000 down payment, but once we used that, it meant that I would barely have two quarters left to rub together. However, God would provide.

I offered a signed contract for $32,000 to the realtor to take to the owner; after some haggling, she accepted our offer and we bought the house. We felt the peace of God as we went through the whole process. We knew that this was the place that the Lord wanted us in. I did not understand at the time, but this would be the area where I would live for eighteen years until the present time.

We got back in the car and drove to Miami with the peace that we had finally found the place where the Lord wanted us to move to. When we got back, I rented a U-Haul truck and went to the storage place where we had our furniture and loaded it into the truck. Then we loaded the remaining items we had in our place into the truck, and we were ready to go. We said good bye to our family one last time.

A Brand New Start

I took my wife, my daughter, our small dog and even our cat and left just as the Lord had told me to. We were hauling my 1991 Honda Civic, so it took us eight hours to get there. When we arrived, it was raining and very late at night, so we just parked the U-Haul Truck in the driveway, took a shower and went to bed. We all slept on the floor that night and we all slept like a baby. Finally we were home.

It took us a while to settle in. Our closest neighbor Nancy was very nice to us, and we quickly became friends. She let me use her mower and trimmer so I could keep the place looking nice until I had enough money to buy one. Everyone was so nice and courteous to us. They would say high to you as you were walking down the streets, and the mailman at the post office even remembered my last name.

Financially though, we were not doing too well. We did not know anybody in the area, and I had no church contacts in that part of the country. I tried to book as many revivals as I could but the pickings were slim, so we tried to make a living anyway we could. I would make cookies and my wife sell them as we went preaching to the different churches. We would sell T-shirts, trinkets, anything to make a buck.

There is an abundance of live oak trees in the area (thus the name Live Oak), so we started collecting the moss from the trees and selling it. However, we soon gave up on that idea as we had to fill a large plastic bag just to make a buck. We started home schooling Charis, with Yvette doing most of the schooling, and I teaching her the math. We had bought her school supplies thanks to donations from the churches.

We would travel together everywhere, and even took our dog Sucha with us. She was a cross breed of Pomeranian and Keeshond, and was easily the best behaved dog we have ever had. She was such a good dog, that whenever I would walk her, I would do so without a leash because I never had to worry about her taking off and running away. One thing she did not like was taking a bath. Whenever we called her saying it was time for her bath, she would go away and hide.

I could share all the horror stories about our ministry travels, especially when it comes to the accommodations. Because many of the churches that we went to minister to were a part of our Pentecostal denomination, they did not have a revelation of grace and therefore did not treat us very well. The offerings were barely enough to help us get by, and many times we had to stay in dingy, dirty places.

One time we stayed in the home of this pastor, but the room we had was very dirty. It had so many roaches walking all over the place that we had to leave in the middle of the night and rent a hotel out of my own pocket. Another time we stayed in a room that happened to belong to a little dog, whose name was, you guessed it, Little Dog. He would try to get into his room all day long, so we had to make sure we kept the door shut all the times.

One day Charis left the door open and he snuck in and got under the bed. We had a time trying to get him out of there, and it took a valiant effort from the pastor to get him out. On another occasion, we stayed with a pastor in Mississippi who had this huge grandfather clock right next to our bedroom. I knew that it was going to give me trouble because I am such a light sleeper. Sure enough, whenever the top of the hour came around, the grandfather clock made a very loud sound.

Finally, when I could no longer take it, I had to get up in the middle of the night and silence him for good. In the morning during breakfast, the pastor noticed that his clock was extremely quiet. When he asked if we had messed with it, I sheepishly confessed to my crime. There was no harm done as he quickly got up and got his blessed grandfather clock working again. After that, I made sure there were no grandfather clocks next to the bedroom where we stayed.

Later that year in the month of August 1992, we went on our first trip to Miami to visit our family. Yvette and Charis would always stay with my in-laws, while I stayed with my parents. It was a good working arrangement, since we did not all fit in either place. Whenever we went to Miami, I took the opportunity to preach in as many churches as I possibly could, since that is where I had all my ministry connections.

While we were still there, a huge hurricane made its way towards the southern part of Florida. In all the 26 years that I had lived in Miami, no hurricane had ever come through or even close to that area. However, I had a strong feeling that this would be the one. At first, it seemed like it was going to go up north like the others but suddenly it stopped and made a sharp turn, as it made a beeline towards Miami.

Hurricane Andrew was a category 5 hurricane, and it was very dangerous. If it kept going in the same direction it was going, it would hit the city of Miami head on, causing severe casualties and unimaginable destruction. I went to prayer that night asking the Lord to turn it away to an area where it would cause minimal damage. I am pretty sure that there were other men of God praying similar prayers in the city.

During that night, Andrew made a slight correction in its path and made landing near Florida City which was sparsely populated.

Although it was hit very hard, there were minimal casualties. The Lord intervened for sure, as this was nothing short of a miracle. Early in the morning I went out and surveyed the damage; there were tree limbs all over the place and several homes were missing tiles from their roofs.

Andrew became one of the most devastating hurricanes ever to hit the state of Florida. We sure had picked a dandy time to come to Miami. As we got ready to go back home, we said good bye to our family, and went on our way. It would be only the first of many trips that we would take to Miami through the years since both of our families were still living in Miami. We usually went at least twice a year to visit them.

My mother's health began to get worse, as she was in the hospital a lot now. I started to witness to her more and more but it seemed the more I tried, the further she withdrew. My father was even worse, as he would not even let me talk to him about anything related to Jesus or the Bible. I became so discouraged about their spiritual condition, that I decided it was time to have a heart to heart talk with Papa.

Chapter 10

HIDDEN IN THE WILDERNESS

It happened later that same year when I was driving back home from Miami by myself. It was a six hour drive, so I had plenty of time to pray and talk to Papa. As I poured out my heart to Him in prayer, I began to feel a strong presence of the Lord inside the car. All of a sudden, I heard His voice as clearly as I have ever heard it. He said to me: "Your mother and your father are in my hand; leave them there".

The peace of God came all over me, and I knew that I had heard from Him. From that point on, I never again talked to them about the Bible or anything related to the gospel. I just began to shower them with love and kindness. He had told me to leave them in His hands, and that is exactly what I intended to do. It took several weeks, but He did not disappoint me. I found out that this lady had moved just a few doors down from the apartment where they lived.

Her name was Blanca (White). She started coming every day to visit with my mom and talk to her about the things of God. This lady was relentless and determined, the kind of person that will not take no for an answer. She became very good friends with my mom and spent a lot of time together. Slowly my mom began to open her heart to the truth of the gospel, allowing me to pray for her and even attending the services when I ministered in nearby churches.

God was doing a supernatural work in her life as her faith was growing daily. In the summer of 1993 during one of my trips to Miami, she was hospitalized. She spent most of the time I was there in the hospital. When it came time for me to leave, I went to the hospital to see her. I kissed her on the forehead and hugged her tight, not knowing that was the last time I would be able to do so. She passed away a few weeks later as I was preaching a revival in Tallahassee, Florida.

She surrendered her life to Jesus a few days before she passed away with Blanca praying by her side. I performed her funeral in Miami with all our family present to give their condolences. I had an opportunity to share the gospel with those that were present, and pray for them. The presence of God was there with me all the time. After the funeral on the trip back home, the devil kept telling me that if I would have stayed in Miami with her, she would not have died.

I am not going to lie to you and say that I was strong and I rebuked him. I cried like a baby under a great amount of guilt and condemnation. The enemy of our souls does not fight fair; he is extremely evil and very wicked. To this day, he still tries to accuse me and make me feel guilty about leaving my parents. But I know in my heart, that if I had not been obedient to the Lord and done what He asked me to do, my mom would never have been saved.

Before I left Miami, I gave my dad a small book as a gift titled "God's Promises", containing many promises from the Bible concerning many different areas of spiritual needs in a person's life. I told him to read the book whenever he felt sad or lonely and it would give him peace and comfort. My mom and dad were real close and they never went anywhere without the other. I knew this was going to be a big blow for him, especially after I was gone and he was all alone.

I had asked my parents several times to move with us to Live Oak, but they had always turned down my offer. I guess they were too old to move, and were used to the warm familiar surroundings of South Florida. As you get older, it is not that easy to pack up and leave your old home to move to a place you do not know, and start all over again. I did not understand them back then, but now as I am in the autumn of my years, I kind of do. Things change as you get older.

When we are young and strong, we have a tendency to be selfish and inconsiderate towards those who are much older and wiser than we are. Young people think they know a lot, but in reality are very foolish. Many times young people get away with making stupid mistakes because of their youth and vitality. They can always start all over again. Older folk can ill afford the luxury of making such mistakes. They do not have the strength anymore, and time is not on their side.

However, by the time you realize your mistakes and are willing to share them with the parents you love, they are no longer here. Then all you have left is a feeling of longing for an opportunity to share these feelings with them. Maybe we will get that chance on the other side, when we finally are all reunited on the beautiful shore. The Lord will dry our tears, and we will have eternity to make everything all right.

A New Beginning

When I got back home, I found out I had received a letter from the headquarters of the denomination I belonged to asking me to appear before the board regarding an issue. I had an idea what this was about. You see, I had never affiliated our church with them, and now the man that I had left as pastor of the church was not even licensed with them. This was more than they were able to bear or even tolerate. However, I was trusting on God to be my defense attorney.

When I appeared before the board, they accused me of stealing money from the church, and interrogated me until they just ran out of questions to ask me. I had nothing to hide, so I answered all their questions one by one. Finally they concluded that the accusations were unfounded. Then they told me that if I wanted to keep my credentials with them, I had to sign a pledge regarding doctrinal and holiness standards which I had refused to sign before.

Even though the majority of the churches that I was preaching at were associated with them, and I knew what it would mean financially to me and my family, I told them that I would not sign the document, and that I was not interested in renewing my license with them. They seemed to be very surprised by my response; however they proceeded to tell me that they would not place any obstacles in my path and would not do anything to hinder my ministry.

Finally, I would be free to pursue the will of God without having to comply with a ridiculous set of man made rules and regulations. However, it also meant that many of the doors that were opened to me before would now be shut. For the next several months, I really struggled to pay all my bills and put food on the table. Before, things were tight, but now I was really facing a dire situation that grew worse by the day.

The Financial Test

During this process, the enemy began to mock me and put thoughts in my head like: "You were once an engineer making a lot of money, and then you gave that up to become a pastor, and now you look at you; you don't even have enough money to put food on the table". He continued to pound me over and over again: "You did not hear God tell you these things, you just imagined it". Many times I thought about getting an engineering job and quit the ministry.

One weekend I was preaching for a church in Panama City, Florida. I had labored all weekend not only preaching my heart out, but also ministering to the people in the church. Many had been healed; several had received the baptism of the Holy Spirit as we had a tremendous move of the Holy Spirit. When it came time for the pastor to give me a love offering, he gave me a check for $100 dollars. When I saw the amount, I became quite upset.

I had labored very hard all week end, and was expecting to be rewarded financially for my labor. Normally people have no compunction in paying hundreds of dollars for their health when they go to the doctor or psychiatrist, but when it comes to giving for spiritual ministry they are stingy. They do not realize that spiritual ministry is the most important type of service they will ever receive in their life. "Let the elders that rule well be counted worthy of double honor, especially they who labor in the word and doctrine. For the scripture says, you shall not muzzle the ox that treads out the grain. And, The laborer is worthy of his reward." 1Timothy 5:17-18

I decided to have a little talk with the pastor about the love offering he had given me. I told him that with offerings like the one he had given me, I was going to have to get a regular job and quit the ministry in order to be able to feed my family. He looked at me insulted and said that when he was evangelizing, an offering of $100 was a good offering. I guess he thought that if it was good enough thirty years ago, it should have been good enough for me. I did not answer him, and just walked away. When I went to pray, the Lord gave me a strong rebuke. He said to me: "Don't you ever beg man again for money; whenever you need anything, come and ask me. I will move on the hearts of those who are my servants, and they will give unto you." Later that year, the Lord gave me a word through a prophet telling me He was going to push away the hypocrites from my life. That word began to come to pass with a vengeance.

A friend of ours from Haiti, who knew of our financial struggles, gave me a card with three words written in real large black letters that said: "WATCH GOD WORK" and she told me to place it in my office where I could look at it every day. I put that paper in my office like she told me, and I would look at it every time my faith began to waver. I have that paper in my possession to this day, and I still look upon it whenever I need faith to have my prayer answered.

I needed a miracle, and I needed it quick. I sought God on my face with fasting and prayer. I knew that He would help me and would not let me down. He had come through for me many times before, and He would do it again. However, the waiting process was getting to be exasperating. Finally one day I was watching a Christian preacher on TV and he was talking about sowing and reaping. Usually I did not pay much attention to such things, but this time it was different.

God was using that man to talk to me directly. I felt His presence so strong, that I quickly took my wife into my office and told her that God had put on my heart to give a certain amount of money a month to a ministry. It was not a very big amount, but to me back then it was a fortune. In the natural it made no sense. If I barely had enough before to pay my bills and eat, imagine now. I knew that I had hit rock bottom and would loose everything if I did not get a miracle.

My wife knew that I had heard from God, so she told me to obey God and do what He had asked me to do. As we made that decision, unexpectedly an extension cord that was lying on the floor exploded, burning a hole in the carpet. There was absolutely no reason for that cord to do what it had just done. It was absolutely impossible for this event to happen, unless it was triggered supernaturally. I knew right away that the devil was mad and had just thrown a little fit.

This act of obedience on my part was the event that triggered a release of the blessings of God on my life from that point on. I had to learn this lesson the hard way on a personal level. Having experienced famine first hand in Cuba, and gone through excruciating situations of great need there had left a mark on my life. I always had a problem with giving; the Lord had to break that bondage from my life, but in order to do it He needed for me to perform an act of faith.

The Training Begins

For the next several years, I would have to be trained for a season to hear and obey the voice of the Lord tucked away in the wilderness, in the backside of the desert, unknown to most people. He had to purge me of religious leaven, wrong concepts and doctrines that had accumulated over the years and had become a part of my mindset. God had to break me and teach me to obey Him, trust and depend on Him, and to walk in brokenness and in humility.

During this season of time, the Lord showed me that His Church was fragmented, impotent, carnal and out of order. The spirit of religion, control, pride and fear, combined with a good dose of ignorance, has stifled the ability of most churches to recognize, train, develop and release potential five-fold leaders, and deprived the people of their God given right to fulfill their gifting and callings in the Body.

I had to let go of old paradigms and man made doctrines that I had learned in the past as I allowed the Holy Spirit to teach me all over again from scratch. As I began to receive only from Him, revelation after revelation began to come into my spirit as I grew day by day in His presence. This developed in me a sharp discernment, so that I was able to discern between the spirit of truth, and the spirit of error.

The Spirit of Truth was operating in me at a very high level, and I would not compromise it for any amount of fame, fortune or anything this world had to offer. The Lord began to give me many dreams and visions, some of them dealing with the end times and the Day of the Lord. Some of them had to do with the changes that were taking place in my life and ministry. He showed me what countries I had to go to, and who I was supposed to bring with me.

He also told me what cities in the United States I needed to go to, and always provided the contacts for this to take place. The Holy Spirit became my closest friend and ally, as He would continually lead me and comfort me during times of grief and loneliness. Unlike man, He never let me down, not once. He is the most faithful and humble being that I have ever met in my life. I do not want to grieve him or in any way cause Him pain. He is very precious to me.

This kind of walk is not easy, and most people are not willing to endure it. It requires complete surrender to the Lord, and the discipline and determination to succeed. The person, who has this type of intimate walk with the Lord, is not going to be a crowd favorite. Most people might even consider him strange, weird or just plain crazy. He does not live to please men, but to please the Lord. These people are rare. They are rejected while alive, and exalted when dead.

This man is even rejected by other good men because he is considered too austere, too committed, too negative and unsociable. He will say nothing that will draw other men to himself, but only that which will draw others to God. He will cry with a passion and say things this generation has never heard, because he has seen visions that no man has ever seen. He eats the bread of affliction daily, but gives the Bread of Life to anyone who will listen.

He will tell you what you need to hear, not what you want to hear. Because of this, this person is despised and rejected by the crowds, but beloved by the lambs of God who are starving for a word of truth; a word from God. The pastors in most churches want the power and anointing that resides in these vessels, but only if they can control it and manipulate it to their advantage. Otherwise, they rather have a suave, entertaining, safe ministry instead.

"And no man puts new wine into old wineskins; else the new wine will burst the wineskins, and be spilled, and the wineskins shall be destroyed. But new wine must be put into new wineskins; and both are preserved. No man also having drunk old wine immediately desires new: for he says, the old is better." Luke 5:37-39

In the following years, the Lord began to open doors and started to connect me with ministries who understood grace, and truly valued the gift that was in me. God began to move in a great way whenever I ministered in those churches. He began to perform supernatural miracles that I had never seen before in our ministry. All kinds of Goiters, Hernias and Cancerous Tumors began to shrink and disappear whenever I laid hands on the people and prayed for them.

I remember one time a man came up for prayer with a huge goiter right in his throat. There was a heavy presence of God in the service that night, and I knew that the minute I laid hands on that goiter, it would be healed. As I laid hands on his throat, the power of God hit that man as he collapsed on the floor. Whenever he stood on his feet again, I asked him to check his throat and try to find his goiter. When he did, an expression of shock came upon his face.

He said: "It is gone; it is not there." Miracle after miracle took place in the revival, as the Lord moved mightily in the all the services. I remember that the people would come up for prayer, and the word of knowledge was so sharp and crisp that I was able to tell them what was wrong with them before they even opened their mouth. Many that had been praying for the baptism of the Holy Spirit were all filled.

The Lord also began to use me to pray for women who were not able to have babies. I remember one time I was in Miami holding a revival for a pastor friend of mine, Mariano Forte. He and his wife had adopted a son because they were not able to have children. One night, as I asked for all the women that were not able to have babies to come forward, she came along with them.

When I saw her come forward, I knew right away she would get her miracle that night.

The minute I laid my hand on her and commanded that womb to open and be fertile in the name of Jesus Christ, she collapsed to the floor. I knew in my heart that the Lord had performed a miracle in her. Weeks later after I had returned home, I got a call from Mariano telling me the news: she was one month pregnant. He asked me to come back to Miami and hold some more meetings for him, this time for a week.

Revival Breaks Out

In that revival, there was an incredible outpouring of the Holy Spirit. Many people were saved, and many healed each night as the Lord confirmed the word with signs following. I remember one night during the revival a drug dealer was present at church. He had been invited by one of the young men who had been delivered from drugs, and he was sitting in the front row. That night the power of God came upon that man, and he was saved and filled with the Holy Spirit.

A couple of days later on Friday, we had the most unusual move of God upon the children. I felt in my heart that God wanted to minister to children that night so I asked them to come to the front for prayer. As I began to pray for them, a most unusual thing began to happen. As I prayed for them, they all began to collapse to the ground speaking in tongues. I did not think much of it, but later something happened.

As I continued to pray for other people that had needs, I noticed that all the children were still lying on the floor crying and travailing in the spirit. This went on for over thirty minutes after which, they all began to laugh uncontrollably. It was a as if an invisible switch had been turned on in the spirit realm. It is unusual for children to be still in one place for such long periods of time; even more so for all of them to begin to cry, travail and laugh all at the same time.

As this was going on, the parents began to approach the altar where their children were with a perplexed look on their faces. I had to talk to them and tell them not to worry, that he children were under the power of the Holy Spirit and that soon they would be back to normal. A few moments after I had spoken those words, the oldest of the children, a young girl about twelve years old, got up and her face was shining with the glory of God. I had never seen anything like it.

As I was about to begin ministering to all the people that by now had flocked to the altar, the Lord spoke to me and said: "You are no longer going to pray for the people; tell the young girl to pray for the people." From experience, I knew better than to argue with the Lord, so I told the young girl that God wanted her to pray for the people. She said: "Me? I don't know how to pray for the people; I have never even prayed for anyone before in my whole entire life."

So, I told her to go lay her hands on the ones that she felt needed prayer, and just pray: "Jesus, please touch them." She agreed and began to move throughout the crowd laying hands on the people and praying for them. As she prayed for the people, many began to weep, others began to repent and surrender their lives to God, while others began to be healed in their bodies. The Lord began to show her who to pray for, as she moved quickly all over the auditorium.

Then, as all the children began to get up one by one, I went to each one of them giving them the same directions I had previously done with the young girl. As all the children began to move throughout the congregation praying for the people, the power of God came down on everyone that was there. Some of the people who were outside in the parking lot, hearing the commotion, tried to get back in the building.

But as they tried to open the door to come inside, they were hit by the power of God collapsing to the floor. As they got up from the floor, they staggered like drunken sailors. I had never seen anything like it in all the years of ministry. We agreed to continue the revival while the fire of God was raging. People continued to come to the meetings, not to hear me, but to experience the presence and power of God.

The revival was stopped however, due to circumstances beyond my control. To this day, whenever we talk about it, he tells me that if I would have told him to, he would have continued the revival. In retrospect, I wish I would have. This type of visitation from God does not happen often; so when it does happen, we must be willing and ready to lay our plans aside, and ride it as long as possible.

Revival continued to take place however, in many other churches that we ministered in. Multitudes were healed of diseases like diabetes, arthritis, lupus, heart problems, cysts, cancer, deafness, glaucoma, cataracts, tumors, lumps and bumps, and all kinds of back problems disappeared when we prayed for them. A woman with a hole in her lung heard about us and came down from Port Charlotte to a church in Miami for prayer and was miraculously healed by the Lord.

She felt fire in her lung burning her and started screaming out loud: "It is burning; it is burning!" In another church a woman that was paralyzed in a wheelchair was healed as she got up when the power of God hit her. I was ministering once in Miami in a church that was pastored by one of my spiritual sons Pete Casanova, and a woman from Brazil who had a cancerous tumor in her vocal cords came up for prayer.

When I prayed for her, the power of God hit her and she collapsed to the floor. However, what happened next I had never seen before or since. As she was lying on the floor, she began to shake and convulse violently in the area of her neck. It looked as if some invisible hands were performing an operation to remove the tumor. When she got up, I had her check her throat to find the tumor; but the tumor was gone.

Addicted to His Glory

We will never know until we get to heaven the impact that those revivals had on the lives of the people that were a part of it. It is the type of revivals most churches desire and long for, but never seem to be able to have. Most people seem to go through life without ever experiencing a supernatural visitation from God. But once you do, you are ruined for the rest of your life as nothing else seems to satisfy your hunger.

Once you get hooked on the glory of God it becomes more intoxicating than any drug, alcohol, food, sex or anything this world has to offer. Nothing else seems to even come close to the thrill, the ecstasy of being in the thick, heavy presence of almighty God. Whenever I preach a meeting, if the awesome holy presence of God does not fill the auditorium, I consider the whole service to be a complete and total failure.

It is a tragic thing whenever people can have church without God's presence and not even realize it. Who needs God in church when you can have a large choir, comfortable seats, a state of the art sound system, fancy lighting and a preacher to feed you a few morsels and make you feel good about yourself. As long as you can keep the people happy, they will keep giving and that's what it's all about. It is not about God at all; it is a business, and it is all about control.

If the Lord were to come and visit many of the churches in the world today, He would probably turn their tables over and say some things to them that I don't think would be very pleasant. We do not belong to ourselves, we belong to Him; and the church belongs to Him, not to the pastor. Until we learn that most valuable of lessons, we will not be able to find favor with God, and walk in close communion with Him.

God is not like man who dwells in a three dimensional world; He dwells in a multi dimensional realm. This is what we call the supernatural realm. We do not have access to this realm except through our spirits by the vehicle of prayer and worship. In essence, our world is made of multiple layers or realms of existence. This has been proven by scientists in recent years and was published in Time magazine just a few years ago. We cannot see these realms unless He reveals it.

Whenever His glory manifests in a place, we experience an invasion from the supernatural realm into our realm; or if you prefer, we could say that we step into the supernatural realm. When this takes place, we experience what is called the manifest presence of God. Any time His glory manifests in a place, anything can happen; no healing is too difficult; no miracle is too great. Nothing is impossible with God.

The scriptures say that the earth shall be filled with the knowledge of the glory of God. Notice it says the knowledge of the glory, not the glory. How does the awareness or the knowledge of the glory of God come? Knowledge introduces us to the glory. Knowledge means to understand and know. It is the exact same word used in the scriptures when it says that Adam and Eve had intimate relationship.

In order to be able to enter into the glory of God we must have an understanding that this glory only comes through intimate communion with the Lord. The Lord is bringing this revelation knowledge of His glory in these end times. In the past, revivals have lasted for very short times. People have seen the manifestations, but they had no knowledge of the glory. When the revivals ended, there was no knowledge of the glory to continue to nourish it.

The people saw the physical manifestation of the glory, but they never entered into that knowledge. It is the same when you give a car to your son. He sees the car and its power, but he has no knowledge of the car. We cannot enter into that dimension of glory if we have no knowledge of what the word glory means. The word glory in Greek is Doxa, and in Hebrew Kavod; Kavod means weighty. When a person speaks and his words are heavy, it is because of the glory.

The word glory means purity, beauty, fame, magnificence, majesty, splendor, holiness, honor, power, riches and grace. The glory of God is the visible and tangible manifestation of all the attributes of God to the five physical senses of men. What is invisible to our eyes becomes visible; what is intangible becomes tangible. That is why Isaiah said that the glory of God shall be seen over us. That means it will be manifested visibly over His lambs in the end of times.

"For, behold, the darkness shall cover the earth, and gross darkness the people: but the Lord shall arise upon you, and his glory shall be seen upon you." Isaiah 60:2

"Will a lion roar in the forest, when he has no prey? Will a young lion cry out from his den, if he has taken nothing? Can a bird fall in a snare upon the earth, where no trap is for it? Shall one take up a snare from the earth, having taken nothing at all? Shall a trumpet be blown in the city, and the people not be afraid? Shall there be calamity in a city, and the LORD has not done it? Surely the Lord God will do nothing, unless he reveals his secret unto his servants the prophets. The lion has roared, who will not fear? The Lord God has spoken, who can but prophesy?" Amos 3:4-8

Chapter 11

THE MAKING OF A MAN OF GOD

It was a lazy winter day in the year of 1995. My wife and I were sitting in the living room talking about life, when my wife says to me nonchalantly: "Don't you feel as if there is something missing?" I responded telling her that I thought everything looked normal to me. Our nine year old daughter was in the den playing, our little Pomeranian dog Sucha was laying by our feet, our cat was in the kitchen, and the two of us were sitting together. Everything was as it should be.

She continued to press the issue however, insisting that she felt there was someone missing. Suddenly she turned to me and said: "Don't you feel as if there is a little boy missing in our family?" The moment I heard those words, a cold chill ran through my body. It had been nine years since Charis had been born. Now we were both much older, and besides our finances were not doing that well; I just could not imagine adding another baby to the equation.

Again, I said to her that I did not belief we were missing a little boy in our family, this time with discernible concern in my voice. We went on to talk about other things and that issue was forgotten. However, a few days later my wife had me pray for this couple who wanted to have a baby and were not able to. She knew that the Lord had used me in the past to pray for barren women, and God had opened their wombs. I had quite a successful track record in this area.

About a month later, we received a phone call from the same woman we prayed for telling us that she was pregnant. She was ecstatic and overjoyed at the news, especially after being told by the doctor that she would probably not be able to have children. Well, that was not the end of the story. A couple of months passed when one day my wife came to me and told me that she was experiencing nausea and vomiting.

I quickly dismissed it, saying that she probably must have eaten something that caused stomach indigestion, or maybe it was a seasonal virus. However, deep inside of me I felt that something was afoot. We decided to go to the clinic and have her take a pregnancy test. As we sat around waiting for the nurse to return with the results, the pressure in the room began to mount as I was perspiring through my hands.

My wife kept staring at me and glancing nervously around the room. Suddenly, the door opened and the nurse walked in. She had a Mona Lisa smile on her face, which was difficult to discern. And then she dropped the bomb, saying to Yvette in a jovial tone: "You are pregnant!" It took a few moments for us to digest this piece of news. We felt like Abraham and Sarah at the time when they had their son Isaac.

Isaac had come at a time when Abraham was a hundred, and Sarah was ninety. We were not that old, but Yvette was hardly at a premium breeding age at thirty four. We thanked the nurse and left the clinic with a sense of resignation, but at the same time great peace. We knew that the Lord was involved in this somehow. When we arrived home, I went to have a talk with Papa about our new baby on the way.

He spoke to me and said that He had sent us that child to be a blessing to us, and that he would lack nothing. He was going to be His servant, just like I was. Then I asked Him what name I should call him, and He quickly gave me the name Benjamin. When I asked Him why, He said because His right hand of power would be revealed to me in the future. He reminded me how He had given me the name Charis for our daughter and how He had later revealed His grace to me.

Of course the name Charis means grace and the Lord did reveal

His grace to me later in her life. Now He had given me the name Benjamin for our son, which means son of the right hand, saying to me that He would reveal His right hand of power to me in the future. I asked Him to confirm that this was the indeed the name that He had given me for our son, by having both my wife and our daughter unanimously agree and approve of the name Benjamin as soon as I told them.

The moment I told both Yvette and Charis the name that the Lord had given me for our son, they unanimously nodded their heads in agreement; acknowledging that they approved of the name the Lord had given me for our son, Benjamin. As we were waiting for the arrival of our son, other things began to happen as well. Yvette's father and mother upon hearing the news of her pregnancy, decided to move up to Live Oak to be with her, and help her through her pregnancy.

We helped them to get settled quickly, and proceeded to show them around the city. They had always loved the city of Live Oak from the very first time they had come up to be with us. They had gotten tired of the crime, pollution and the high cost of living there. They were moving from the fourth largest metroplex in America (behind New York, Los Angeles and Chicago) with a population of over five million people, to a city with a population of just eight thousand people.

We tried to make the transition as smooth as we could for them, but they got used to their surroundings rather quickly. Many Spanish people had begun to slowly move into the area in recent years, and now there are two Cuban restaurants as well as a couple of Mexican restaurants in the city. Also, as you go to the supermarkets you can see much more Spanish products on the counters. This sure has helped to make them feel much more at home.

On April 21, 1996 my son Benjamin was born in the early afternoon in Shands Hospital in Gainesville. I was there with my wife every step of the way through the birthing process, the same as when Charis was born. Benjamin was born very healthy, and when I held him in my arms I felt the presence of God come all over me. This child was indeed sent from the Lord; now I knew then that everything was going to be fine.

My First Prophetic Rap Music CD

In the fall of 1999, I was sitting in the living room with my twelve year old daughter Charis having a father/daughter chat. Then suddenly out of nowhere, I began to receive words to a song in the form of rap music. Now, you need to understand that I had never written any music songs before; Rap or otherwise. This was a brand new experience for me. I quickly told Charis to get me some paper and pen so I could begin to write down all the words that I was receiving.

As I began to write down the lyrics to the song I was receiving, more and more began to flow. It seemed as if I had tapped into a creative part of me, which for some reason had been activated by God. A strong prophetic anointing began flowing through me, and I intended to flow with it no matter where it took me. Charis joined into the flow, as she also began to receive words to the song. Before long, I had written my first Rap song of the CD titled Bone to Bone.

The prophetic anointing continued to rest upon me, as I wrote one song after another. But then, I began to think about what I was doing and it did not make sense. I did not have a studio to produce these songs, nor the money to pay a studio to do it. However, I did know one thing; and that was that the Holy Spirit had initiated this, not me. I knew that if the Lord was in this, He was going to have to provide a way for me to be able to do this.

Later that same year during a trip to Miami, God spoke to my spiritual son Pete Casanova and told him to give me his computer. When he told me about it, at first I was reluctant to accept his offer because he was not doing well financially and he had just gotten that computer. But he insisted telling me that God told him to give it to me. Finally, I realized that God was in it, and that his act of obedience would result not only in a great blessing for me, but for him as well.

I am a dinosaur when it comes to technology, and now I was given a computer that I neither asked for nor wanted. So I began to learn how to use it through the long, arduous process of making mistakes. Then I found out that a new software technology had just come out in the market that would allow me to produce music using my own computer. I became ecstatic at the realization that I would finally be able to produce the music for the songs that I had written.

I purchased the music software, and slowly began to put together the music to the songs, one by one. I asked God to give me the wisdom to be able to do this, and to provide the music loops for me to be able to do it. CD's containing music loops easily sell for over $50 each, and I was going to need many different types of loops to produce my album. It was going to take another miracle from God to achieve this, as I did not have the finances to do it. Once again, God provided.

I was able to download free music loops from different websites here and there as the Holy Spirit continued to guide my every step. The free music loops I was able to get, were exactly the ones I needed. Slowly but surely, I was able to get enough of them to produce my first song, Bone to Bone. After the first one, it just became easier to do. Finally, after much work, I finished all the songs. All I needed now was to record my voice in a studio and this thing would get done.

The Lord provided that as well for a very reasonable price, and I was able to produce my first CD Bone to Bone. When I was recording my voice at the studio, the guys there asked me who had helped me with the music. When I told them that I had done it all by myself, they were astonished and could not believe it; they told me that my music was the best they had ever heard that was not done professionally.

Afterwards, the Lord opened the faucet wide open as He kept giving me more songs. Many songs were prophetic in nature as they dealt with future events; others had to do with real life issues, while others had to do with Bible stories. All of them contained the gospel in some way, and have been used by the Lord through the years to touch countless lives. I am yet to find a person, young and old, who does not like our music and has not been impacted by it.

My Dad's Conversion

I kept traveling to Miami to visit my dad and do ministry there for some years after my mom passed away. I noticed that he kept the book of God's promises that I had given him next to his bed on a night stand. I could tell he read it often by the book marks he had inside. Whenever I was there with him, I tried to help him out anyway I could. I would clean the house, do groceries and other things that he could not do.

As he got older in his mid eighties, the cataracts in his eyes did not let him see very clearly, so I started cutting his hair, and even shaving him. On December of the year 2000 during Christmas, I noticed that he was nearing his day of departure. He was weaker than usual, and the spark was no longer in his eyes. I sat next to him in the sofa as I discerned that the time had come for him to be saved.

I told him that his time to depart this earth was getting close, and that he needed to get ready for it. I told him that I loved him and wanted to spend eternity with him and mom in heaven, but that he needed to take a step of faith and be obedient in order to do so. I asked him if I could lead him in prayer to receive Jesus as his savior. He agreed so I led him in a prayer of repentance and salvation.

Then I told him he needed to be baptized in water. My dad had always rejected any talk of baptism, but this time he nodded in approval when I asked him. I filled the bath tub in his apartment with warm water, and proceeded to place him in it. As he sat on the tub and made a declaration of his faith, I baptized him in the name of Jesus Christ as I put him under the water. When he came out of the water with his hands up praising the Lord, his countenance shone with God's glory.

I could not believe what had just happened. The Lord had answered my prayer of many years, and now my father was gloriously saved. All of this had been done in stealth mode, so as not to give the enemy the slightest opportunity to stop it from happening. The glory and the peace of God were all over my dad's face. I had never seen him so happy in my entire life, not even when we finally managed to get out of Cuba and come to the United States thirty seven years ago.

Two weeks later on January 10, 2001 while I was home, I received a phone call from my brother Mario telling me that he had taken my dad to the emergency room. I immediately got in my car and drove down to Miami. After driving six hours non stop, I got to the hospital where I met my brother who told me they had just taken him into the emergency room after making him wait all day. When they brought him back out, he was unconscious and on an artificial respirator.

He never regained consciousness; he passed away in the morning of 1/11 at 11:11 am. My brother took care of all the funeral arrangements with the money that my dad had in his bank account. We attended his funeral with a few people in attendance, and later proceeded to a local cemetery where his body was laid to rest in a plot of land he had purchased years before for my mom and him. I knew that I would see him again in heaven, but his departure hit me very hard.

My father and I had become very close through the years, and as I went back to his apartment, the grief I felt was very overwhelming. I had never felt this deep sense of loss, not even when my mom had passed away. Many friends of mine in the ministry tried to comfort me to no avail. Then a couple of days later, as I was getting ready to wrap things up and return home, an Indian mailman came knocking at the door.

He was dressed in shorts, wearing sandals and his body was covered with perspiration. When he asked me about my dad, I told him that he had passed away a couple of days earlier. He then proceeded to try to comfort me, which made me somewhat irritated. This Indian man, who probably was not even saved, was attempting in a feeble way to comfort a man of God. I tried to dismiss him when I heard the voice of the Lord say to me firmly: "Shut up, and listen to him."

I obeyed God and kept quiet as the mailman continued to speak to me comforting words. However, the words coming out of his mouth were no longer his words. It was as if the Lord was using him to speak to me such words of wisdom and divine love that I had never heard before. As I continued to listen to what he was saying to me, the words that were coming out his mouth began to comfort me, and great peace came all over me. I will never forget what I learned that day.

The Lord indeed taught me a valuable lesson by showing me that at a given moment in time, He can use anyone or for that matter anything that He sees fit to bring about His will upon the earth. In the past, He spoke to Balaam through his donkey, and He spoke to Moses through a burning bush. The Lord has spoken to me in the past through unsaved people, bums, my wife, TV set, children and sometimes even through my mother in law. The Lord has a great sense of humor.

Many times we will miss God if we are not sensitive to His voice and the moving of His Spirit. Actually, it is very easy to miss if you are not where you should be in your relationship with the Lord. What would happen if you were to be walking one day and you saw a burning bush? Would you even stop to check it out? Or, would you think that maybe God is trying to say something to you? I think most people would go right on with their lives, without giving it a second thought.

Sailors, Eskimos, farmers and animals in general are far more sensitive to what is going on around them in nature than most of us who have become disconnected from God's creation and our surroundings. Most animals somehow know when there is about to be an earthquake, a tsunami, tornado and even when it is going to rain. They will let you know by how they react, and certain things that they do. Dogs have a sense for danger, and the ability to discern evil intent.

If you listen to their barking and pay close attention, they will let you know what it is they are saying. In some cases, dogs have saved the lives of their owners, and even alerted their owners whenever there was something wrong with their health, when doctors were not able to tell. Talking about God using the foolish things of the world to confound the wise; I have for sure seen my share of them.

1 Corinthians 1:27 "But God has chosen the foolish things of the world to confound the wise..."

The Emergence of a Man of God

As the years went by, I continued to travel throughout the States; mostly in the eastern part of the country with the exception of Texas, and Idaho in the Pacific Northwest. For some reason, I have not been able to go to the West Coast of the country, however I believe that in the very near future the doors will open there so that I may share the word that the Lord has given me for this end times. The people in that part of the country need to hear this word from the Lord.

I also began traveling overseas to various countries. The doors for me to go to Cuba opened in 1996, and I have been going there ever since. I have traveled to the provinces of Villa Clara and Havana. We helped another ministry for five years to establish a work there, and now we are working to establish an independent apostolic church in Alamar, with a group of men who are hungry for training in the apostolic and prophetic. Cuba is a needy and difficult mission field.

We also were invited to go to Mexico and conducted some revivals there in the cities of Campeche and Merida. We had the opportunity to minister to many Mayan people, as well as those of Mexican ancestry. The Lord also opened a large door for me in the country of Honduras. We went to the city of Comayagua in the southern portion, as well as the cities of La Lima, San Pedro Sula, Progreso and Villanueva in the area of the north. We conducted revivals in all those cities.

We also conducted many seminars during our trips there and taught in a Bible School operated by MUNA, the ministry we work with whenever we go to Honduras. We also were interviewed by ENLACE during one of our trips, the Spanish TBN in Central America, and was shown all over the nation of Honduras and other Spanish speaking nations. Like in most countries in Central America, Honduran people are spiritually rich, although most of them live in poor conditions.

The Lord opened doors for us to go into a High School in La Lima and do our Rap Music for the students there. I was allowed to talk to them about Jesus Christ, and even minister to them during an altar call. There were over three hundred students in attendance and most of them really enjoyed it. About fifty of them came and gave their hearts to the Lord with tears in their eyes. Some of them were hit by the power of God collapsing to the floor. They had never seen it before.
What a contrast to America, where I have also been to the schools ministering to the children, but have never been allowed to use

the name of Jesus Christ. No wonder a deep gross darkness has begun to settle over most of the nation. We have been blessed to donate hundreds of our Prophetic Rap Music CD's to the children in Honduras and America, as well as to drug and alcohol addicts in Rehab Centers.

God began to give me dreams and visions of the night showing me that I was a prophet of God. Slowly, He began to confirm my calling as I began to be recognized throughout the United States and overseas, as a prophet of God. He began confirming my ministry with abundant miracles, signs and wonders. Our prophetic words began to come to pass as I continued to travel to the same places through the years.

We began to give words of knowledge to people that were very sharp and accurate, at times even discerning the names of people, their jobs, hobbies, gifting and even things that they were dealing with. Sometimes, diseases that the people were suffering from were revealed and healed instantly as we declared it over them. I have always had dreams and visions of the night, but around the turn of the century I started having many dreams about future end time events.

Some of them have already come to pass, while many of them have not taken place yet. The next chapter contains all the dreams and visions that the Lord has given me over the last several years which are not personal in nature. They are also posted in our website for everyone to see. There is one that due to its sensitive and controversial nature had not been released. However, after holding on to it for almost five years, I feel the time has come to release it in this book.

As I endeavored to be faithful to the heavenly calling that God has placed on my life, and labor in the office that He had called me into and confirmed in many nations, He then slowly began to deal with me about other things. I started having visions of the night, dreams and different experiences where the Lord was showing me walking in a higher level of ministry and anointing. They are very personal to me and I am not at liberty to share them; however, they are real.

I have never sought any titles, or called myself by any titles. The only thing I desire is to be a servant of the Lord and to see His glory. However, in many of these dreams and visions of the night, God began to refer to me as an apostle. Years later, I began to be recognized as an apostle not only in this country, but also overseas. When He began to show me this, I did not even know what an apostle was. I had to research the topic to understand what He was showing me.

I am considered an apostle by many churches, and when I am with them I function in the office of an apostle bringing spiritual impartation to them as well as apostolic applications. Many churches see me as a prophet, and when I am with them I function in the office of a prophet, ministering in the realm of prophetic revelations. If a particular church needs revival, then I function in the area of evangelism bringing salvation, deliverance and outpourings of the Holy Spirit.

I have served as pastor and teacher to a church for seven years while we were in Miami, Florida. However, now I pastor other pastors and help them in whatever area they need help with. Having been a pastor once, I feel compassion for them. I see so many pastors with such a great need for someone to come alongside of them and just be a mentor to them; someone they can turn to when they go through a real rough patch, or when they are facing a real difficult situation.

One of the greatest needs in the churches today is for the leadership and all the lambs of God in general to be trained and prepared for the work of the ministry. We need for every single member of the body of Christ to come into alignment and begin to function as God intended for them to. They all have different talents and abilities that need to be discovered and activated so they can begin to be a blessing to others.

There are those who may not feel a call to ministry, and not everyone is going to be in the five fold ministry. Everyone is however, called to a life of prayer. Not everyone is going to be a natural intercessor, but every one can intercede. In our book Open Heavens, we cover the topic of intercession in great detail. I encourage everyone who reads this book that you try to get closer to the Lord while there is yet time.

We all see through a glass darkly, and as we get closer to the appointed time, we will begin to see and understand clearly things that we were not able to see before. When the Lord called me out of the church I pastored in Miami, and said He had a work for me to do, I did not understand Him. But now after many years, God's destiny for my life is finally becoming clearer. I do not know everything that the future holds, but I do know that it is going to be glorious.

www.ingramcontent.com/pod-product-compliance
Lightning Source LLC
Chambersburg PA
CBHW061729020426
42331CB00006B/1157